Funded by

MISSION COLLEGE
Carl D. Perkins Vocational and Technical Education Act Grant

the **method** method

the

method.

method

7 obsessions

that helped our scrappy start-up
turn an industry upside down

ERIC RYAN
+ ADAM LOWRY

with Lucas Conley

portfolio / penguin

This book is dedicated to all of the *People Against Dirty* who made Method possible. To our team members who have given us ten great years of unwavering passion, courage, and hard work, to our advocates who brought Method into their homes and helped spread our revolution, to our families who never laughed at us and who made personal sacrifices to support our dreams, to the investors who put their money where their mouth was, and to every retailer who supported Method by putting our little bottles of goodness on their shelves. This book is for you!

INTRODUCTION

HELLO. AS YOU PROBABLY GUESSED FROM LOOK-
ing at the cover, this is a book about Method, that quirky, California-
based maker of environmentally friendly and stylish cleaning products
for the home. But before we get all excited to share all about what goes on
behind the scenes here (but sorry, we can't share the photo booth pictures from
last year's prom), you should know that this is much more than our story. *The
Method Method* is packed with innovative ideas about business—the very same
ideas that led to our ranking as one of *Fast Company*'s and *Time*'s most innovative companies in the world, earned us a spot on the Inc. 500 (we reached number
seven), and won us a PETA Persons of the Year award, among closets full of other
design, sustainability, and product awards. (Forgive us for bragging, but our editor said this would give us more credibility). Tips, case studies, favorite quotes,
embarrassing mistakes—we gathered everything we've learned in ten years
of building our brand and crammed it all into these pages. In the process, we
learned something new, too:

Everything we know, we learned from you.

It's true. Just by picking up this book—if you haven't bought it yet, go
ahead . . . we'll wait—you have joined a community of millions of customers who
engage with our brand every day, teaching us how to do our job better in so
many different ways. And we've been listening. In just ten years, you've helped
us grow Method from a two-man, four-product outfit operating out of the back
of our car into an international brand at the vanguard of a new category of envi-

ronmentally and socially driven companies changing how business is done. So, yeah, we owe you one.

Taking stock this year on our tenth birthday, we decided to show our appreciation by sharing everything we've learned in one nice little package. The good stuff, the bad stuff, even the proprietary stuff that made our lawyers squirm. We're not worried that you're going to steal our ideas and go try to mimic us—we trust you, and besides, our obsessions are easier said than done. We do hope that, no matter what industry you're in or what position you hold at your company, you'll be able to learn something from our ideas and possibly make them your own. We also hope you'll be able to avoid some of the mistakes we've made—and trust us, we've made plenty.

At the core of it all are our seven obsessions, the rules we live by. Other businesses might refer to these as strategies, but *strategy* is a tired corporate word for something you do for your boss. Obsessions are bigger. Obsessions are something you take home with you, something that drives entrepreneurs to think deeper, work longer, and change entire industries. Some we've followed from the beginning; others we've learned the hard way. Reflecting on the past ten years, we understand now that our obsessions are actually rules written by our younger selves, holding us to the ideals we shared when we first decided to launch the company.

It hasn't always been easy. Consider our competition: Soap companies were the world's first multinationals and the first to pioneer mass media ("soap opera" anyone?). Not only did they have a hundred-year head start on us, they had tens of thousands of employees and millions of loyal customers on their side! People told us we were committing entrepreneurial suicide, but we saw plenty of room for improvement in this rather stagnant industry, and so we decided to take it on. To succeed, we knew we couldn't launch just one groundbreaking innovation or change just one rule—we had to redefine the battlefield as much as possible, turning their weaknesses into our strengths. They have size and power, but we have speed and agility. They follow Six Sigma, but we built an imaginative, irreverent culture that allows our people to create and express themselves through their work. They try to be all things to all people, but we inspire a small group of advocates dedicated to evangelizing our brand to anyone who will listen. Devoting one chapter to each of our seven obsessions, we explore why they matter, how we live up to them, where we've gone astray, and what we've learned from each along the way. Admitting that we could never have done this without a lot of help and inspiration, we also spotlight someone (our "muse") in each chapter who embodies each obsession even more than we do.

If you're like us, you're impatient to revolutionize the way business is done and to create positive social change in the process. Maybe you're a business leader—the MBA searching for ways to put your new ideas into practice. Maybe you're an aspiring entrepreneur—itching for an opportunity to disrupt an industry. Whether you're sitting in a cube farm at MegaCorp or in your underwear in your garage, we know where you're coming from because we've been there, too. Take it from us, change is possible—as long as you're ready to obsess over it.

Never before has the world of business evolved as quickly as it's evolving today. It's not just technology—everything about the world of work is changing: the ways in which we design, produce, ship, and sell goods; the means by which we find, gather, and share information; and how we assess value—not only on our balance sheets, but in our personal and professional lives. Each of these areas presents profound challenges to today's entrepreneurs, and each of our obsessions is designed to help you meet those challenges and exploit the cultural shifts behind them.

We hope the lessons in this book—real, unvarnished, battle-tested tales gleaned from years of outthinking our bigger and better-financed competitors—will help inspire you to see your job differently. We hope this book will help lay a path from the way most of us work today to the way we could work tomorrow—a model that aligns business interests, social interests, and environmental interests. We also hope this book does right by our partners, team members, and customers, celebrating them while attracting new allies, talent, and advocates in the process. Finally, we hope it makes our moms proud.

If this book does nothing else, it should dispel the myth of the lone entrepreneur. Our names may be on the cover, but what's inside represents the enormous efforts of loyal colleagues inside and outside Method, past and present. Getting this far took a lot of help from a lot of people, and to all those who helped us become what we are today, we are grateful. We couldn't have done this without your passion, long hours, personal sacrifice, courage, and heavy doses of weirdness. Thank you, people against dirty!

—Eric and Adam, friends and founders

CONTENTS

the **method.** method

OUR STORY

THE FIRST
TEN YEARS OF
MAKING SOAP

from a dirty apartment to soap star

WE PROMISED THIS WOULDN'T BE A BOOK ALL about us, but in order to understand where we're coming from and the principles that drive our company, a little background is in order. Method's story begins in 1998 with a chance encounter between the two of us on a crowded flight from Detroit to San Francisco. Old acquaintances from school in Grosse Pointe, Michigan, we fell into easy conversation. While we'd sailed together on Lake St. Clair as teens, we'd gone our separate ways after high school—Adam, to the world of equations and fluid dynamics studying chemical engineering and environmental science at Stanford University, and Eric, to the University of Rhode Island and London's Richmond University, where he spent five years testing the patience of his business and communications professors. As we'd only seen each other on holidays over the years, it wasn't until that plane ride that we realized we were both living in San Francisco.

Heading back to California on that late-night flight, we discovered we were both at a point in our careers where we were asking ourselves, "Is this really what I want to do?" Working on climate research, Adam had grown weary of the environmental echo chamber. Compiling data for the Kyoto Protocol was compelling, but how fulfilling could it be if the only people reading his work were already convinced the environment was in danger? Working for advertising agencies, Eric could feel himself growing jaded. Most of the work he did never saw the light of day, killed by uncreative clients in bad golf shirts. And while crafting ad campaigns for brands like Saturn was fun, how was he supposed to stay engaged after it became obvious his only job was to sell a mediocre product— not help make it any better? As the two of us caught up, one thing became clear:

we were both looking to create something different and pursue our entrepreneurial aspirations. But what?

We had plenty of ideas—a modern interpretation of Pottery Barn? A healthy
pizza chain?—but none of them were very compelling or made much sense.
Though we left the plane without any great ideas, we were excited by the prospect of doing something truly different and worthwhile. A few months after
reconnecting, one of Adam's roommates got married, so Eric moved in and our
ambition to start something grew by the day. But *what to start*? Every bar-stool
brainstorming session led us to the same conclusion: Keep our day jobs. But as
it turned out, it was Eric's day job, which included creating a new toothpaste for
a major brand (because the world *really needed* another toothpaste brand) that
led us to our eureka moment. After spending countless mind-numbing research
hours in supermarket aisles, Eric found himself imagining how he'd reinvent some
of the products we use every day. He realized that rather than trying to create
something out of thin air, it was much easier to find a proven but tired industry
and identify a way to disrupt it. This is how you are trained to think in advertising:
Look at a category and find the cultural shift or consumer motivation that the
leading brands are not delivering on. The space in between is where you'll find
the opportunity.

A few months later, we were both home in Detroit over the holidays and
headed to northern Michigan for a weekend of skiing. During the five-hour road
trip, Eric mentioned that the cleaning products industry might be the right place
to dig. From Eric's point of view as a marketer, the cleaning category looked like
a sitting duck. Think about it: The household cleaning aisle is huge, but every
mainstream product more or less looks the same (like a relic of the 1950s), positions itself the same ("Cleaning will be a jiff!"), and works the same (with enough
toxic chemicals, who can't get grass stains out of a T-shirt?). As a chemist, Adam
saw vast room for improvement among the "green" alternatives—at that point,
a handful of pious brands selling subpar products under the auspices of conser-
vation and personal sacrifice. From our perspective, shopping for soap was like
dating in a town with two options: Hire a so-called professional (a sure thing,
even if it leaves you feeling dirty) or get stuck with a prude (and embrace auster-
ity in the name of moral righteousness). Frankly, the choices sucked!

Yeah, we know. It sounds weird: two twenty-four-year-old guys not known
for their home-cleaning habits idling away the hours lost in conversation about
dish soap and disinfectant spray. But it didn't *feel* weird. On the contrary, it felt
perfectly natural. Rather than design one innovative product, why not disrupt an
entire category? The more we talked about it, the more convinced we became

▲ **FIND THE CULTURAL SHIFT.** Our methodology for disrupting mature categories.

that cleaning products offered the ideal opportunity to combine our passions and skills. Eric imagined bringing style to the category. If you could transform a cleaning product for the house into an accessory for the home—offering a playful piece of sculpture, say, in place of a plain old soap pump or spray bottle—people might just be inclined to leave it on the counter instead of hiding it in a cabinet or tossing it under the sink. Adam imagined bringing substance to the category. If you could replace the toxic ingredients with natural stuff that worked

THE POWER OF THE DUO

Look at any great company and you will find a combination of diverse skills, often springing from a pair of diverse leaders. Mickey Drexler and Don Fisher at Gap, Steve Jobs and Tim Cook at Apple, Steve Ballmer and Bill Gates at Microsoft—some of the most original ideas are the offspring of two opposite perspectives. Of course, many great companies are launched and run by someone flying solo, but it can only help to have a partner who complements your skills.

▲ **THAT'S NOT BEER.** Fortunately, our products are nontoxic, so no roommates were hurt in the making of this business.

well and smelled nice, people might feel better about what they were using in their homes (and the impact it had outside them). It was the first and most powerful "yes, and" conversation in Method's history—our "peanut butter and chocolate" moment where everything just came together. Here was a major, mature product category that had completely missed two profound cultural shifts. Bringing style and substance together could potentially revolutionize the industry and change people's entire attitude toward cleaning. After five hours discussing the idea in the car, we arrived at the mountain more excited about soap than skiing.

A few days later, after talking things over on the chairlift, we returned to San Francisco and launched our research phase. This was about when our roommates began suspecting we were nuts. What exactly was in all those beer pitchers labeled DO NOT DRINK? Why the sudden interest in cleaning the toilets so often? Every trip to the grocery store became a reconnaissance mission. Every weekend errand, a market feasibility study. Hashing out our observations week after week from our modest (and, ironically, very dirty) apartment at 1731 Pine Street, we reached a couple of what Eric would call key consumer insights.

CULTURAL SHIFT #1: LIFESTYLING THE HOME

Eric's advertising background helped us see that even though the leading cleaning brands marketed their products like commodities—simple utilitarian solutions to use, throw under the sink, and forget about until the next cleaning day—consumers actually invested a lot of interest and emotion in caring for their homes. After all, our homes are extensions of ourselves. Moving into a new place, we pore over every last paint swatch and carpet sample. Settling in, we build fond memories of and strong feelings for every last mismatched coffee mug and hand-me-down end table. This cultural shift was increasingly evidenced by the explosion of shelter magazines, shows like *Trading Spaces,* and entire networks like Home and Garden Television. More than in previous generations, people were envisioning their homes as personal expressions. Home fashion and design was taking hold in the mainstream. No longer were consumers satisfied with Aunt Sophie's old dining room table and other passed-down relics—they wanted that chic new Seabury sofa from Crate & Barrel. And once they updated the couch, suddenly the rug looked tired. Then the window dressings, too. Accessorizing and stylizing the home with designer goods became a national obsession, giving rise to major chains like Pottery Barn, IKEA, and Room & Board.

The cleaning industry missed this shift entirely, positioning their products as solutions to everyday problems rather than complements to a lifestyle. Just as Vidal Sassoon and Williams-Sonoma identified ways to bring aspiration and a premium appeal to previously boring, solution-focused mass categories like shampoo and cookware, we saw an opportunity to leverage design and emotion to elevate the banal household cleaner into an accessory for the home.

So why is it—if we care so much for our homes—that we leave all the upkeep to that motley crew of uninspired jugs and spray bottles lurking under the sink? Tapping our expert research consultants (i.e., our friends and families), the answer was inevitably the same: Nobody really wants to think about cleaning products. At least, we try not to. Whenever they come up, we tend to regard them as a necessary evil—quick solutions to annoying problems. Granted, cleaning products should be easy, but couldn't they also be pleasant to look at or even fun to use? What if we were to design products worthy of a place on the counter, ones that we actually looked forward to using? This insight led us to our first mission: making cleaning fun.

Tapping Adam's chemical engineering know-how, Eric was shocked to find how "dirty" the cleaning products on the market really were. Essentially, we were using poison to make our homes cleaner, surrounding ourselves with toxic ingredients and polluting our environment in the process. Worse, few consumers knew how bad it was. We'd been bamboozled into believing that the acrid whiff of bleach was the smell of "clean" and that the burning under our fingernails after scrubbing the counter was "hygienic." It didn't make sense to us that we pollute when we clean and use poison to make our homes healthier.

The second cultural shift in the category was that the consumer was putting more emphasis on natural health. Living in San Francisco at the time, you could see the natural and organic movement moving into the mainstream from a mile away. Yet while consumers were buying organic milk and strawberries in droves, they were still spraying pesticides throughout the kitchen in the form of antibacterial cleaners. We felt it was only a matter of time before consumers would care as much about what they put on their skin and in their home as they did about what they were eating and drinking. Sure, cleaning should be thorough, but

---

A NAMING METHOD FOR NAMING METHOD

It's a question we get all the time, and a valid one for any entrepreneur: "How do you come up with a name for your company?" Eric's background in branding and name development taught us to start by selecting a "jumping-off word," something that captured the spirit of the idea we wanted to communicate. In our case, we wanted to represent a whole new approach to cleaning—a smarter, more holistic process—a new way, based on great technique rather than brute force. *Technique* became our jumping-off word, and one evening while we were both in the bathroom brushing our teeth (yes, weird), Adam threw out the suggestion *method*. Eric yelled out, "That's it!" and we had our name. Claiming a common term hasn't exactly been easy (our lawyers advised against it), but we believe the name has made a difference in the success of the company, and we couldn't imagine it any other way.

---

shouldn't it also be healthy and safe? What if we were to design nontoxic products that didn't leave a legacy of pollution? This insight led us to our second mission: making cleaning actually . . . clean.

THE ELEVATOR PITCH: AVEDA FOR THE HOME

We said we were both searching for "something different" when we ran into each other on that plane back in 1998. When we sent out our first business plan, eighteen months later, we finally began to understand what *different* was actually going to mean. Picture the scene: It was early 2000, the NASDAQ was north of five thousand, and everyone and their kid sister in San Francisco had a dot-com dream. Sneaker millionaires were springing up as fast as you could say "first-mover advantage," lavish launch parties were the norm, and we were running around town with an earnest vision for soap.

Welcome to the proof-of-concept stage of a new business, the phase where you strap wings to your back and try to convince others to jump off a cliff and learn to fly with you. Before long, our roommates weren't the only ones who thought we were crazy. A cleaning products company founded on high-end design and an ethos of sustainability? Venture capitalists laughed off the idea. "Green" was a niche for puritan do-gooders willing to put up with substandard products. And design? When it came to washing hands and doing dishes, people only cared about function and price, not aesthetics.

It wasn't that we hadn't thought things out. To the contrary, we'd spent months honing our pitch before shopping it around. Our big idea—to bring a personal-care approach to cleaning—was clear and simple. "Aveda for the home"—a nod to the botanically based high-end beauty brand—was our pitch-perfect elevator pitch. The problem wasn't communicating the idea; everybody we approached understood what we were trying to do. The problem was, *no one thought we could do it.*

Maybe you know the feeling—that diffuse sense of panic that someone, somewhere, is about to steal your idea. In our case, there were seven multinationals with names like P&G and Unilever dominating this space. With their thousands of employees and millions of dollars poured into market research every year, how could they possibly miss the opportunity we saw? This scared us to death; there must be something we were missing if no one before us had done this. Then again, IBM missed Apple, Kodak ignored digital, and nobody knew

▲ **TWO FRIENDS WITH TWO VERY DIFFERENT PHILOSOPHIES.**
The birthplace of Method, a very dirty San Francisco flat.

more about coffee than Maxwell House, but they didn't see Starbucks coming. Big brands miss big opportunities all the time, and despite the skepticism, we still believed we had a great idea.

This is the awkward and insecure stage that makes getting companies off the ground so damn difficult. It's also where most business dreams die, only to be occasionally eulogized when a friend or family member asks, "Hey, whatever happened to that crazy idea of yours . . . ?" The fundamental problem at this stage is that you need money to launch the business and prove the concept, yet who's going to give you money when you haven't proven the business idea? This is the point when you find out how bad you want it, how thick your skin is, how much you're willing sacrifice to make it happen. You have no choice but to prove the business yourself and do it as quickly as possible with what little resources you have.

To get Method through the proof-of-concept stage, we crafted a plan to create a first line of products and distribute it to twenty local stores. The idea was to prove we could compete against the national brands—even with no employees, no salaries to support ourselves, no previous training, and with a very small amount of savings. We knew success during this stage was dependent on our ability to get others to share our vision and support it (either with an immediate cash investment or a pledge to help with some part of the business). Luckily, we were fortunate enough to get suppliers, designers, lawyers, accountants, manufacturing partners, and friends to offer free services in exchange for equity or payment—assuming we raised money down the road.

Over the next six months, we created our first line of products through a lot of quick experimentation and a heavy dose of borrowed expertise. Working on the formulation, Adam was able to convince local chemist Steve Deptris and the Royal Chemical Company to help us create and manufacture our formulas. We strived hard for nontoxic products that actually worked—no easy feat. Meanwhile, Eric focused on the product design and brand identity. Our first bottle was inspired by a camping fuel bottle found in Norway, and we convinced Michael Rutchik, a local designer, to partner with us on the graphic design. To help the bottle stand out on the shelf and reinforce our safe and human approach, our labels featured photographs of people cleaning the appropriate surface. The essential skill at this stage: infect others with your vision and passion. Make your mission contagious so that others will take risk and work with you, even if it's for very little up-front compensation.

With finished products in hand, we started the uphill climb to get them into stores. We can still remember walking into that first grocery store at 6:00 A.M., tracking down the manager, and launching into a nervous thirty-second pitch about why he should carry Method. We're still not sure why he said yes—was it the beauty and appeal of the product, or just his concern that we would keep coming back? Regardless, on February 28, 2001, Method landed its first sale at Mollie Stone's Market in Burlingame, just south of San Francisco! Imagine our feeling of awe as we watched the cashier scan our product right before our eyes: The bar code lined up, the register beeped, and the Method brand was born.

Over the next several months, we went door-to-door, pitching to every Bay Area independent market we could find. We settled into a routine, picking up product at the factory in the morning, delivering it to stores throughout the day, and counting up how many we sold by day's end so that we could build a sales story. To market the product, we held in-store demonstrations and passed out coupons, which also doubled as consumer research. Not only did sales start to pick up, but the product began striking an emotional spark with consumers! Our customer service number (actually Eric's cell phone) was on the back label of every bottle. As e-mails and calls of praise started to pour in, the business came to life. Consumers were raving about our unique products, like the cucumber bathroom spray cleaner. At first, we were sure it was our friends playing practical jokes on us, but (after hanging up on the first few callers) we realized our customers were actually excited!

Within a couple of months, Method products were available in thirty stores, and our confidence was building. But in order to keep growing after maxing out the number of local independent grocers, we knew we would need to start selling to bigger retail chains like Safeway or Albertsons. Fortunately, all that time spent getting our hands dirty (figuratively of course) was finally paying off; after months of selling directly to independent store managers, we were actually beginning to understand the ins and outs of the grocery industry. More important, we had some real sales data now, so we could actually sit down with the big buyers and properly pitch our line with some hope of getting in.

But we had one big problem. Our seed money was gone, and selling to grocery chains would require ramping up our inventory and shipping directly from a warehouse rather than hand-delivering product out of the back of Adam's mom's car. We needed a lot more capital, and while our proof of concept was strengthening, it was not strong enough to raise investments from venture capitalists or other professional sources. Despite our early success, we needed to make a big leap—and quickly!

Now, like it or not, the only way to get through this awkward entrepreneurial stage is to raise "angel" money (you could also call this part the Friends, Fools, and Family stage). Angel investors get their name for one obvious reason: they save you from death (or delay it, to be more precise). We set out to raise capital from anyone willing to believe in us—who in the end turned out to be our families, roommates, and a handful of friends. While everyone gave small amounts, it was enough to sustain the business and keep us on a path toward our next milestone: proving the business in major grocery store chains.

Many entrepreneurs struggle with the decision to take money from close friends and loved ones. The reality is that you don't have much of a choice. Before you've proven your idea, the only thing people can bet on is you . . . and, inevitably, the only people willing to do that are your friends and family. Of course, the upside to taking money from the people you care about most is that it puts a lot of pressure on your back. (No, seriously, this is a good thing.) You go from not wanting to let yourself down to not wanting to let your family down. It forces you to do everything you can to avoid sitting down at Christmas dinner saying, "Sorry, Grandma, I lost that ten thousand dollars you loaned me."

With friends-and-family money in hand, we finally achieved our goal of getting Method into the bigger grocery store chains—among them, Ralphs in Southern California and QFC up in the Seattle area. But while the business was growing, it was also burning through cash faster. Soon, not only were we working 24/7 to expand distribution across nearly two hundred stores and counting (a full-time job in and of itself), but we also began trying to raise professional money—venture capital. We were going big or going home.

This is the point where we should probably say something gritty and inspiring about triumph through ingenuity and perseverance. But the fact is, we were laughed out of every venture capital pitch meeting, we ran up $100,000 of credit card debt as the angel money ran dry, and after we quit our jobs to chase this harebrained idea, Eric's girlfriend dumped him. And that wasn't even the low point. Lower still were the nights waking in a cold sweat, fretting about how to pay back the money we had borrowed from our friends and family. Even lower was the spiraling nausea of nearly losing our first round of venture capital funding when the economy took a dive in 2001. (After all, who would want to invest in premium home cleaning products during a crippling recession?) At that point, our vendors began putting us on credit holds, freezing our production, and send-

▲ **GET YOUR HANDS DIRTY.** There is no substitute for hands-on learning by doing the selling and delivering yourself. (Adam holding our first invoice and Eric performing an in-store demo. Don't ask why we are in the liquor aisle.)

ing us scrambling to find a bridge investment. The lowest moment? Viewing a car accident as good luck because—with just $16 left in the bank—we could use the insurance payout to cover our rent and food.

Unlike most business success stories, this one fully acknowledges the role that *luck* played in tipping the scales. As when David Bennett, cofounder of Mollie Stone's Market, suddenly decided to buy all the home-brewed spray cleaner we'd managed to squeeze into our car. Or when the president of a major gambling company in Las Vegas floated us a bridge loan just big enough to keep us alive until a pair of enterprising VC investors named Steve and Herb Simon decided to risk half a million dollars on a pair of unproven kids in the midst of the (first) global financial meltdown of the century.

Ultimately, Eric got the girl back, Grandma didn't lose her nest egg, and the insurance company didn't ask too many questions. From the beginning—and at so many other points we'll never have the time or space to tell—luck often made the difference between success and failure. That said, the old cliché is true— sometimes you have to create your own luck. The recipe: a dash of opportunity and a whole lot of preparation. Getting a new venture off the ground requires busting your ass and envisioning multiple ways to win. Just remember to bring a valid credit card to the celebration dinner. Ours all got denied. Luckily, when we told the owner, a friend of ours at San Francisco's Caffe Sociale, why we were celebrating, he let us off with an IOU.

AIMING HIGH: SETTING OUR SIGHTS ON TARGET

Of course, luck only goes so far, and at some point, you have to rely on ingenuity and perseverance to make up the difference. Our lucky break with the Simons had only postponed the most dire financial consequences. (We know what you're thinking: *How much was that celebration dinner?*) While the first $500,000 check from the Simons was more money than either of us had ever seen, more than half of it went straight to impatient suppliers, overdue bills, legal fees, and an ever-expanding—albeit exceedingly friendly—phalanx of VC contract attorneys. As the champagne fog cleared from our heads the day after our fete at Sociale, we realized what was really giving us indigestion: With just $200,000 left in the bank, in order to continue our partnership with the Simons, we had ninety days to expand distribution to eight hundred stores.

Here's the deal: professional investors need to draw a line in the sand, to set some type of milestone that gives them the freedom to step away if things aren't moving in the right direction. Investors need safeguards to keep from indiscriminately pouring money into well-meaning but money-losing enterprises. Sure, your cousin's idea for an automated toaster-size olive press in every kitchen may be compelling, but at what point do you stop sending him checks and cut your losses? In our case, if we wanted the second half-million from the Simons, the contract stipulated that we had to ramp up distribution from two hundred stores to an astounding eight hundred in under three months.

The problem with such an aggressive distribution goal is that it creates an unhealthy incentive: any store at any cost. Inevitably, you wind up putting yourself in stores you shouldn't be in. But we didn't have time to sweat the details.

With just ninety days to achieve our goal, we abandoned every other activity and became full-time salesmen—knocking on every grocer's delivery door and competing with each other to see who could sign up more customers at retailing and natural-products conferences. Having exhausted the network of independent retailers in our area, we had started approaching buyers at the regional chains—Wegmans, Albertsons, Safeway—meeting after meeting, sharpening our pitch each time. As fast as the distribution agreements stacked up, however, our cash vanished faster.

It wasn't as if we were paying ourselves lavish salaries (or any salary, for that matter). We both believe strongly in investing in talent, so the two of us had been deferring our own salaries to pay our consultant, Alastair Dorward, competitively. But at the close of our Series A, we'd hired Alastair full time. The only one of the three of us with an MBA and real-world entrepreneurial experience, Alastair was worth every penny. But as our accounts had increased, so had our overhead—staff, rent, and operating costs were burning up more of our capital every day. Meanwhile, the rejections added up, the money dwindled away, and we got increasingly desperate—both at work and at home. Soon enough, we were back in the poorhouse, and our roommates were once again balking at covering our bar tabs. Grandma couldn't help us now. The only way forward was to scale up—dramatically—and the only way to do that was to land a national distributor.

From the very beginning—before we had any products to sell, before we'd even named the company—getting our new cleaning products into Target had been our ultimate goal. Not only was Target our best chance at mainstream credibility, it was a natural fit for our nascent brand. First off, Target was trend-forward. The retailer had already brought beautiful design into the home with designers like Michael Graves and Todd Oldham, and its "Expect more, pay less" motto was an obvious match for our style-plus-substance philosophy. And when it came to national distribution (something we'd promised the Simons), none of the other usual suspects were a good match. Kmart was flailing, and, in 2002, Walmart just wasn't the right place for a premium, design-based start-up to debut. No matter how we looked at it, we were destined for Target.

All of which is to say that, while the Simons may have lit a fire under us, we'd been networking furiously for a Target contact since our fateful ski trip, inquiring through friends, friends of friends, friends of acquaintances, friends of complete strangers . . . and at long last, we received our first promising lead in the fall of 2002. A manufacturer owned by a friendly VC fund was scheduled to discuss a private-label partnership with Target's head buyer. Were we interested in piggy-backing and making a quick pitch after the manufacturer was done (if there was time)? It wasn't the dream date we'd imagined, but a review with Target's head buyer was too tempting to pass up. Accepting the invitation with gratitude, we circled the day on our calendars in red ink.

It's difficult to justify in retrospect, but we were feeling halfway confident about our upcoming blind date with America's third-largest retailer. Devoting our time to closing hundreds of minor sales had boosted our confidence to an all-time high—and not without reason. In the weeks leading up to our rendez-vous in Minneapolis, Target's home base, we'd signed our biggest account yet (a two-state deal with Albertsons, the regional grocery chain), reached our goal of eight hundred stores (miraculously—and recklessly, as you'll see), and trig-gered the second half of our venture capital funding. We knew convincing any-one to take us national with only one product (our spray cleaner in four different variants) wouldn't be easy, but what choice did we have? In the rush to build our distribution, there simply hadn't been time to develop any new concepts. No matter: Our bank account was flush, our supply lines were overflowing, and our pitch was laser sharp. Setting our sights on Target, we actually liked our chances. Luck had gotten us this far, right?

Our chances, as it turned out, were less than those of a snowball in hell. At least, that's how Target's divisional head put it after a cursory look at our presenta-tion materials. Our product was ordinary. Our brand wouldn't have broad appeal. Go home. After weeks psyching ourselves up for our all-important pitch, we couldn't believe our ears. The buyer seemed annoyed with us for wasting his time.

We'd aimed high, failed big, and crashed hard. Going back to work was the worst part. We didn't want to be just another minor-league company stuck in some regional niche, neither growing nor shrinking. (Even if we'd settled for the minor leagues, sooner or later one of the big global brands was going to catch on and copy our model.) After months of seemingly boundless success,

Method had come to a screeching halt. We couldn't help asking ourselves, *What was the point?*

When you're in an entrepreneurial funk, you wind up questioning everything. What am I doing? How on earth did I think I could do this? Do I even want to do this anymore? Wallowing in this kind of mood, you start to think about all the opportunities you passed over along the way. Sometimes it was just an itch—perhaps a casual inquiry about job opportunities during lunch with an old colleague. Sometimes it was a fever—such as the overwhelming urge to drop everything, book a last-minute flight, and start over in some far-off, exotic corner of the world where no one knows your name. We were no different. This was—to put it mildly—a *delicate* phase in Method's history. It all could have gone one way or another.

HAVE THE RIGHT PEOPLE TO LEAN ON

When the going gets tough, especially early on, leaning on people who've been there before makes all the difference. These trusted advisers can be found anywhere, but the closer they are to you the better. We found just such a person in Jim Merlo. Jim is the CEO of one of our first suppliers, Trifinity Partners. Jim and his team were miracle workers, always willing and able to work with us to try something new. Jim, in particular, was the perfect blend of puckish ingenuity and unvarnished honesty. A proudly old-school Chicago manufacturer, whenever we had a problem Jim had seen it before—and "had a guy" who could take care of it. One day when it seemed like we weren't going to pull another rabbit out of our hats, Jim turned to a rather dejected Adam and, in his heavy Chicago accent, said, "Adam, just remember: we're not saving lives here. We're just makin' soap." Merlo's lessons have stuck with us. Always keep your mission squarely in your sights and strive for it like your life depends on it. But when times get tough—and they always do—have someone like Jim around who will take you for a beer and remind you that, luckily, it's not really a life-or-death situation.

THE FIRST SNOWBALL

No matter how much we tried to distract ourselves in the wake of Target's rejection, we couldn't ignore the fact that, without a national retailer, it was only a matter of time before our money ran out, our investors walked away, and everything came crashing down around us. To compete against Goliath, we needed scale, and Target was the best fit. There was only one option: regroup and take another run at Target.

Our first pitch had taught us that Target simply wasn't interested in our modest product line or our relatively unknown brand—yet. So we attacked the obstacles with zeal. Our spray cleaner wasn't intriguing enough? We designed an entire line of home cleaning products! Our brand wasn't famous enough? We enlisted the star power of Karim Rashid, one of the world's best-known industrial designers, commissioning him to create new bottles! We weren't worth the head buyer's time? We found time with somebody else!

Ask anyone in the retail business, and they'll tell you the same thing: Never, ever try to make an end run around a buyer. Even if you succeed by convincing some executive to intervene and put your product on the shelf (unlikely, at best), you'll have made the buyer an enemy for life. Nevertheless, when an old advertising-industry friend of Eric's offered to make an overture on our behalf, we happily allowed him to get us another meeting. Knowing full well what we were up against, he put a call in to the retailer's marketing department and said the magic words: *Karim Rashid*. Within minutes, we had a date on the books: April 10, 2002.

For those who aren't familiar with him, Rashid is the rare designer who believes in creating for the majority rather than the minority. He made his name transforming everyday products—the Oh Chair for Umbra, the Garbo Wastecan, perfume bottles for Issey Miyake—into icons. In short, Target wanted Rashid, and we were just along for the ride. And the ride wasn't free. Hiring Rashid to sketch up our designs and attend our pitch meeting exhausted the very last of our operating capital. This was going to be our Hail Mary pass, an all-or-nothing gamble for Method's survival.

The prototype—a bottle shaped like a bowling pin and cleverly designed to dispense dish soap through a valve in its base—arrived by FedEx just in time for the meeting, led by Eric and Alastair (Adam was scrambling to develop the prototype back in California). Simultaneously relieved and anxious, we filled the bottle with soap (not knowing if it would even work), filed into the packed conference room, and flashed a quick glance over our audience. Glaring right back at us, arms crossed, was Target's head buyer.

Mustering all of his willpower, Eric launched into his presentation—stilted at first, but gathering confidence as he explained our vision for the future of cleaning and home care. Naturally, we came prepared with product sketches,

▲ **PUTTING IT ALL ON THE LINE WITH DESIGN.** Our first attempt at disrupting dish soap, designed by Karim Rashid.

mock-ups of potential in-aisle displays, and a theoretical marketing campaign, but—pinned down by the withering glower of the head buyer—Eric couldn't tell if any of it was hitting home. That is, until he watched the prototype bottle making its way slowly around the room. Reaching the head buyer, he picked it up skeptically, squeezed a stream of soap out the bottom, and exclaimed in wonder, "Oh my god, even I would use this!"

There are a few distinct memories after that—the senior marketing director declaring our product "on trend" and "perfect for Target's guests" (*guests* is Target-speak for customers), the room breaking into applause as we wrapped up our presentation, the head buyer agreeing to a ninety-day, hundred-store trial run—but the rest of the meeting is mostly just a dizzy, elated haze. An hour later (celebrating in a downtown Minneapolis bar), Eric and Alastair called Adam with the good news.

THE SECOND SNOWBALL

Back in California, Adam had been taking care of all the day-to-day operations: formulating the new product compounds, logging the shipments, engineering the Karim Rashid designs. Standing in a friend's backyard when the call from Minnesota came through that Friday evening, Adam could hardly make out what Eric was saying over all the hooting and hollering on the other end of the line. Pressing the phone to his ear, bits and pieces started coming through. "Target said yes" . . . "a hundred stores in Chicago and San Francisco" . . . "June 28th." The blood drained from Adam's face: The upside-down bottle was just a proto-type, built from a malleable aluminum mold and quick-dry adhesives. It wasn't production ready. Even if he started the production process the very next morn-ing, it would take months before the bottle was ready for market. Hell, the lead time on an injection mold alone was six months! But here was Method's crack sales duo, celebrating over cocktails after agreeing to the impossible: a multi-state retail test for a product that didn't exist, in less than ten weeks. Landing their biggest sale yet, they had effectively doomed the company. It was impos-sible. Outrageous. There was simply no way it could happen.

But, it *had* to happen.

Given a snowball's chance in hell, Eric and Alastair had somehow managed to land a deal with one of the world's largest retailers. Now it was Adam's turn to beat the odds. Hanging up on Eric, he immediately dialed Craig Sawicki, Method's manufacturing partner. Sawicki was Alastair's perfect foil. Whereas Alastair was British, refined, and always impeccably dressed, Sawicki was a salt-of-the-earth type who'd spent his entire career chain-smoking in the bowels of Chicago's industrial factories. Reaching Sawicki on his cell, Adam explained the situation. This was Method's chance to break through; everything was on the line. Meeting at Sawicki's office the next morning (after a red-eye to Chicago), they got right to work.

In the days and weeks that followed, Adam and Craig called in every last favor and twisted every last arm on the North Side of Chicago. If a supplier balked on the phone, they would show up at his factory and ask in person. If a fabricator had problems with a particular part, they worked alongside him late into the night to solve the issue. As Eric and Alastair worked the phones and crisscrossed the country in search of new business, Adam and Craig were hun-kered down in run-down factories and grimy machine shops.

Maybe it was because we were too naive to know that what we were asking for was absurd. Maybe it was because we were always willing to work as hard as or harder than anyone we worked with. In the end, it will always be a mystery to us why Craig was willing to pull out all the stops and give up all those nights and weekends for a pair of idealistic kids from Michigan. But he did—and as a result, we met our deadline with Target.

After a mad dash to fabricate and fill thousands of orders by the deadline, our idiosyncratic, upside-down bottles landed on Target's shelves on August 1, 2002. Suddenly, what had seemed bold and revolutionary in a designer's artfully rendered sketch began to feel like a colossal mistake. Standing shoulder-to-shoulder with familiar brands like Dawn and Palmolive, our bottles clearly flouted every rule in the CPG (consumer packaged goods) handbook. The accepted dish-soap doctrine was to use the bottle as a billboard to attract attention in the aisle, resulting in flat form factors and large, loud labels. Ergonomics (how well the bottle functioned) and aesthetics (what it looked like on the kitchen counter, not the aisle) had long been ruled "secondary design criteria." Not only was our bottle aesthetically striking and ergonomically innovative, the label was more akin to that of a perfume bottle than the garish fifties-era bottles shouting for the customer's attention. Instead of an evocative brand name—like Joy, Cascade, or Sunlight—the label read simply, METHOD DISH SOAP.

Intrigued by the funky bottle, unique scents, and minimalist label, some shoppers bought the product on impulse. But while our sales figures were low, the response from those early adopters was encouraging. Letters started showing up at our San Francisco office. Did we make an all-natural shampoo? What about a line of nontoxic laundry detergents? Seduced by our style, consumers were becoming smitten with our substance! (Our employees later dubbed this Method's Trojan horse effect.)

Besides slower-than-expected sales, there was one other small problem: The bottles were leaking. Whether attempting to pop the cap in order to smell the fragrance, or simply curious about the mechanics of the weird-looking bottle, consumers were prying the bottoms loose and then returning them to the shelf, where they proceeded to drip over the entire Method display and pool in the aisle. While a tamper-resistant sticker would later solve the problem, this did not make for a good first impression with consumers or with Target. Armed with a store list, we abandoned our sales work and spent weeks navigating the suburbs of Chicagoland and Northern California (before GPS, mind you), visiting store after store to wipe up the gooey, sticky mess again and again and again. Sisyphus had nothing on us. As we watched our weekly sales start to fall, our hearts sank. No matter how many coupons we passed out, no matter how many store managers we pumped up, no matter how many messy shelves we cleaned up, each week came up far short of the goal we needed to hit to go national. Out of sheer desperation, we even started buying product ourselves and passing it out for free in the parking lots to Target customers (who must have thought we were bonkers). It wasn't our proudest moment, but at that point we would have done anything to ensure our company survived.

Just as we were beginning to get desperate about our underwhelming sales, a new buyer took over our category for the chain. She was intrigued by our products and passionate about our mission. Instead of dismissing the test as a failure, sending us into a death spiral, she dug deeper into the stats—the sales "hurdle" we had been given was erroneously high and there was more to the story. While our unit sales were lower than that of many established brands, we were helping Target bring in new customers and driving greater overall profits for the entire category. When we returned to Minneapolis for our September check-in meeting, Target made it official: We were going national!

When Method's hand soap, our third product, launched the following spring, decorating the nation's kitchen countertops and bathroom sinks with a multicolored array of teardrop-shaped bottles, we had finally become too big for the big brands to ignore. Stirred by the excitement we were generating in the market, century-old brands roused themselves from decades of complacency and began responding with modern-looking, natural products of their own. At this point, we truly understood the multiplying effect of our mission and our belief in leveraging business as a social-change agent. One idea, nurtured by two guys, had grown into three product lines, dozens of retail partnerships, thousands of loyal customers, and millions in sales. More than a personal obsession, our style-and-substance philosophy was becoming a movement.

THE BIG SCALE-UP

Once we went national, the real growth began. Landing in Target gave us credibility to crack other national retailers throughout the United States. We continued to expand the product line to keep up with our consumers' desires for more Method in more parts of their homes, eventually making the leap to Canada, Europe, and even parts of Asia. (Admittedly, in part we just wanted to be able to use the phrase "We're huge in Japan!") Revenue soared, growing 50, 100, even 200 percent a year. Keeping up with our growth meant scaling quickly, and demonstrating scale was critical to proving we were an enduring brand, not a fad. We were overwhelmed with new employees, new partners, new infrastructure, and new ways of doing business (all of it learned on the job, of course). Outgrowing our original office in a Victorian house on Union Street in San Francisco, we moved to a second location down the street. Before long, we were moving again—to our current location on Commercial Street—and opening offices in Chicago and London. By 2006 we were the seventh-fastest-growing private company in the country, according to *Inc.* magazine. And we were doing it in consumer categories that had been flat or in decline for a decade or more.

This was a magical period when we operated the business with an entrepreneurial mind-set and our employees had a high degree of freedom to pursue new business opportunities. Within a few years, we started a show on HSN (the Home Shopping Network), launched an automotive brand called Vroom, created a entirely new body-care line, and launched an air-care line, which included our first foray into electronics. Nothing scared us, and the company approached every project with a can-do attitude. This wasn't your typical start-up growth; this was wild, uninhibited growth—the kind that affords all sorts of insights along the way (as we'll discuss later) and the kind that—at least temporarily—hides all your sins and bad habits (we'll get to those, too).

TURBULENCE DOESN'T MEAN YOU ARE GOING DOWN

For those of you who have studied entrepreneurship, it should come as no surprise that our biggest mistake was simply growing too fast and trying to do too much. Rapidly expanding into a number of areas, we grew naively, as if the good times would never end. In 2008 our mistakes started catching up with us. Ironically, that same year we hit the $100 million revenue mark after doing business for just 2,861 days, or a little under eight years. We reached this goal in less time than Powerbar, Ben & Jerry's, Nike, or Snapple.

Then we hit the perfect storm. Our first major product failure—an ill-advised venture into personal care called Bloq—coincided with a faltering economy and surging oil prices that threatened to further undermine our profitability. At the same time, Goliath woke up, and several of our competitors launched green products that took dead aim at our shelf space and came armed with marketing budgets fifty times the size of ours. (We later learned some of the companies launched these under the code name "Kill Method"—yikes!) Increasingly exposed, we were at risk of becoming a cliché—a premium, high-water brand

▲ **OWNED AND OPERATED BY HUMAN BEINGS.** Blurring the lines between our personal and professional lives rebalances life.

marooned by the recessionary low tide. We had successfully scaled up the business to $100 million at a record pace, but the reality sank in: To survive the recession and get Method to the next stage, we would need to change the way we operated. And do it fast!

Unlike just about all of the previous challenges we had faced, we were now too big to simply will ourselves to success. We couldn't just roll up our sleeves and work a little harder to solve the problems that we were facing. We needed to make some major cuts if we wanted to survive. These were grown-up problems with no easy solutions. And no matter how we crunched the numbers, we were facing every entrepreneur's worst nightmare: laying off colleagues who were more friends than employees.

We've always been open about our finances, and everyone on staff had known for months that we'd have to make cuts, but it was all somewhat abstract until we started naming names. That was truly agonizing. There's no greater test of an owner or manager than when you have to take someone's job—especially after experiencing all the rewards that come with creating those jobs. Without exception, the hardest thing we've ever had to do was take those jobs away. To this day, we remain deeply sorry that we had to do it, and we vowed never again to put ourselves or our colleagues in the same position.

Our culture helped us survive this period. After our departing colleagues removed their photos from the photo wall—our version of the family portrait—and everyone helped them pack up their desks, we all went out and had a drink together. It is in times like this that we truly appreciate the genuine strength of our culture (an obsession you'll hear more about in the next chapter). As each person left, every one of them heading home to break the news to their families, they looked us in the eye and told us they were sorry for what we were going through. Believe it or not—and we hardly could—they apologized to *us*. They felt they'd let us down as much as we felt we'd let them down. Having built the company as a family, the two of us had handled everything personally. Our employees understood what the necessity had done to us. While it probably sounds strange, we believe we're better, stronger people, and better, stronger leaders, having gone through that process.

In just twelve months, we killed two major product lines—body and air care—that had accounted for 15 percent of our business, laid off 10 percent of our staff, changed CEOs to bring in more operating experience, and said good-bye to our most unprofitable retailers. There was not much to be proud of, but if we're proud of anything, it's that we ripped off the Band-Aid quickly. Some companies retreat awkwardly for years, waddling gracelessly as they adapt to a new environment. But as the downward trend in late 2008 stretched from months into quarters, we resolved to get through the pain fast.

ONWARD AND UPWARD

The layoffs knocked us down for a while, but the stability that came as a result has encouraged people to reengage and enabled us to begin growing again—albeit in a far more disciplined way than we did in the past. On a certain level, today's 20 percent growth rate seems relatively placid, but we're different now—both as individuals and as a company. As we write this, we've been in business for more than ten years, emerged from the recession, built a stronger business, and reached record profitability. Though we had to change the way we operated in order to scale the business to the next level, we never abandoned our core values, obsessions, and beliefs. Recognizing the power of our obsessions after they helped us thrive through unprecedented challenges—and how many of our failures could be attributed to straying from our obsessions—only further reinforced them.

We've changed from seeing ourselves as doers to seeing ourselves as leaders. And as leaders, we have committed ourselves to saying what we intend to do and then doing it—setting the right expectations and delivering on those expectations. Leadership can be less concrete than cooking up cleaning formulas and hitting our sales targets. The obstacles are softer, more subjective. The problems are nebulous, easy to miss, and hard to articulate. In the beginning, challenges like launching that first upside-down soap bottle were clear and present. There was a romance to them because there was a job to be done and we knew what it was, even if not exactly how to do it. Now we understand that the job will never be done. It's a different way of thinking about work—an approach that draws on everything we've learned in ten years of business to deliver revolutionary performance with a purpose. It's our way of doing things. It's the Method method.

obsession

CREATE A CULTURE CLUB

use culture as a competitive advantage by branding from the inside out

IF YOU WERE TO ENTER THE METHOD OFFICES AT 637 Commercial Street in downtown San Francisco, walk past the guard dog (a green plastic pooch in the lobby), skirt the security perimeter checkpoint in the lobby (staffed by different team members each day), and penetrate the top-secret defense measures (so secret, there aren't any), you would find yourself at the heart of Method's headquarters—the nerve center where our products are designed and our decisions are made.

There, scrawled across a series of floor-to-ceiling whiteboards we call wiki walls, you would see our strategies, a detailed breakdown of everything we plan to accomplish over the next eighteen months. Our sales goals and financial forecasts, our media plans and product development cycles—all our whats, whens, and hows for the next year and a half, right there in erasable marker. The long lists of statistics and projections would all seem fairly familiar to an executive from any other company . . . all except the section titled "People and Environment."

Culture, as we refer to it informally, has a place on the strategy wall because it's the driving force behind everything we do. In fact, while few modern companies go to similar lengths to foster and measure it, culture is increasingly the driving (or draining) force behind everyone else's results too. While there are as many definitions of culture as there are companies, to us culture encompasses the shared values, behaviors, and practices of a company's employees. To put it another way, it's the code for how we all treat one another. Our goal was to create a culture that would inspire and enable us to do our best work while fostering a workplace that enriches our lives. A great culture is one that's aligned with the missions of the company, be it delivering superlative customer service (like Zingerman's Deli in Ann Arbor), driving innovation (like Netflix), or being a low-price leader (like Southwest Airlines).

Most leaders underestimate the power of culture for reaching business goals, particularly when starting with limited resources. They'll say, "Fix the business first, and then we'll have the time and money to invest in culture." That's like a coach saying, "Once we start winning, we'll get everyone motivated and playing as a team." It just doesn't work that way.

TRANSPARENCY, AUTHENTICITY, AND CULTURE IN AN ALWAYS-ON WORLD

It's a little-known fact that the 1908 Model T averaged 21 miles per gallon (according to Ford's Web site). It would stand to reason that, a century later, automakers would have steadily advanced fuel efficiency ratings to grand new heights. Such is not the case. The big automakers' average in 2010 was 25 mpg—a measly 4 mpg improvement over more than a century, and the minimum required by law. While their advertising campaigns proclaim their commitment to innovation and the environment, auto industry lobbyists and lawyers are hard at work in Washington fighting efforts to raise fuel-economy standards. Though this type of corporate hypocrisy may have flown in the past, we are entering a new, transparent world where the consequences of saying one thing while doing another are beginning to exact a toll on businesses in the marketplace. As founders of our own company and the guardians of a thriving brand culture, the significance of this profound shift in consumer power and priorities was forever on our minds.

Today's corporations operate in an era of unprecedented transparency. The line separating public image and private behavior has all but vanished, eroded by the availability of information and the advance of social media. Pinstriped CEOs rub elbows with rank-and-file shareholders on Twitter; blue-collar factory workers publish candid blog posts about life on the shop floor; fervent brand advocates respond to customers about that morning's company news before the PR reps even hit the snooze button. No longer can corporations afford to talk out of both sides of their mouths, preaching one message to consumers while practicing another behind the scenes. In today's always-on business environment, authenticity is the universal language of successful organizations.

The nucleus of that authenticity—that binding energy generated by employees, customers, and the media alike—is a company's culture. Unbounded by cubicle walls or HR handbooks, culture is the x factor, the soul of the brand, the whole that's somehow greater than the sum of its parts. In contrast to other critical corporate assets, a vibrant company culture doesn't show up on a balance sheet. It cannot be inventoried, valued, or written off. Despite its nebulous nature, not only does everyone tend to agree on what makes a strong corporate culture, we canonize the best examples. Magazines rank corporate cultures in annual lists. Consultants celebrate cultures at industry conferences. Culture is the subject of seminars, books, and entire university courses. Why? We're glad you asked.

Below, a few reasons why you should give a damn about culture.

BECAUSE WHEN IT COMES TO INNOVATION, CULTURE WINS OVER PROCESS Process is about getting where you want to go quickly and reliably (think Six Sigma, business process reengineering, etc.) while innovation is about reaching new and uncharted territory. In our surplus economy, success depends on creating brands and products that stand out, and such innovations are best delivered through open, collaborative cultures. The only way to predictably reach the unknown is with the right culture. Take Google, for example, which is famous for giving its best engineers one day a week to devote to their own pet projects and has beta-tested and launched hundreds of innovative products and services through their Google Labs division as a result of this freedom.

BECAUSE WORD TRAVELS, AND SO DOES TALENT The talent war is heating up, and the winners will be those who deliver a great culture for their employees. According to the Bureau of Labor Statistics, today's average worker changes jobs every 4.1 years. In a media-saturated world, we all hear stories about companies, like the grocery chain Wegmans, that go above and beyond to support and encourage their employees. Whether your culture rocks or is on the rocks, your reputation will precede you. In an increasingly mobile society, the strongest employees need compelling reasons to stay.

BECAUSE THE LINES BETWEEN OUR PERSONAL AND PROFESSIONAL LIVES ARE BLURRING We spend the majority of our waking lives at work, and the texts, e-mails, and calls keep coming long after we go home. We are forever tethered to our jobs, allowing our professional lives to seep into our personal ones. Even our escapism is work-related! *The Office, Mad Men, The Apprentice*—our society is obsessed with workplace culture. There's no escaping work, so the best way to achieve work-life balance is to find a great professional culture that you don't mind letting bleed into the rest of your life.

BECAUSE STANDARDS FOR CULTURE ARE RISING Back in the day, a "casual Friday" policy and some corporate swag around the holidays were enough to stand out from the crowd when it came to culture. Not anymore. Companies like Pixar offer employees over one hundred courses through an internal Pixar University. Zappos offers new employees $3,000 to quit after their first week—97 percent like the new job so much they turn down the offer (and the ones who accept it probably wouldn't have been a good fit anyway). These days, fostering an exceptional culture requires effort and creativity.

For those companies fortunate enough to possess one, a winning culture provides seemingly endless benefits—from boosting employee satisfaction and retention rates to fostering a cohesive brand identity and a high degree of innovation. Companies with resilient cultures attract better talent, inspire more customers, and outlast their competitors.

Most important, a powerful corporate culture offers the ultimate competitive advantage because it's impossible to copy. Trade secrets can be stolen, best practices mimicked, but the many variables that factor into a company's culture—the odd habits of its working atmosphere, the peculiarities of its various hierarchies, the way everyone just gets along—coalesce into that "certain something" that cannot be replicated. Not by competitors seeking to duplicate it, and not by those unfortunate companies who let it slip and then struggle in vain to re-create it once it's gone. Yet by January 2006, we were on the verge of becoming one of the latter.

CAUSE FOR CELEBRATION

By January 2006, Method's success had far surpassed even our wildest expectations. We could hardly believe our good fortune. In just five years, we had become an industry sensation. Our artful designs and environmentally friendly products were all over the press—the brand had become an instant media darling. Our soaring growth, meanwhile, made us the envy of every competitor. We even had invites to the Playboy Mansion (only one of us swam in the grotto, but we'll leave it to you to guess who). Method was the world's first hip home-care brand, and we were making our presence known.

As in each of the previous four years, 2006 ushered in a new round of record-breaking sales figures and a flurry of headlines to accompany them. Our overall revenue had more than doubled the previous year, rocketing past $32 million.

▲ **LIVING OUR VALUES.** As PETA Persons of the year we always make our stance against animal testing clear. Even at Hef's house

Liquid detergent, up over 300 percent for the year, had cracked the industry top ten. Even some of our slower categories, like air care and dish soap, managed to increase sales by 200 percent or more. Sales, buzz, game-changing innovations—no matter how you looked at it, the brand was red-hot.

But with success came a whole new set of challenges. To keep pace with soaring demand, we evolved rapidly. New product lines were springing up as fast as we could imagine them, expanding the brand aisle by aisle and store by store to different corners of the market. New hires swelled our ranks, their makeshift workspaces overflowing into hallways and conference rooms. In the mad dash to keep up with staggering growth, we outgrew our home office three times in five years. New manufacturers, new suppliers, new distributors . . . we were bursting at the seams with start-up enthusiasm.

So why did we feel as though we were on the verge of falling apart?

Josh Handy, Method's Disrupter (aka vice president of innovation), sums it up well: "Everyone you met loved their job and the company so much, they evangelized it to a point of weirdness. But we were in danger of losing one-to-one personal contact—where individuals could affect the direction of the company and where everyone shared the work."

From tense intraoffice e-mails to fewer after-hours jam sessions, the reality was sinking in: Success was changing our culture. We knew our culture was our most valuable asset—it was the reason our employees came to work early and stayed late and the reason the best people in the industry defected from coveted jobs at stable competitors like P&G, Unilever, and Clorox to join us—but we had always thought it was something that happened organically, a serendipitous accident that arose when all the right forces converged. We'd never really thought about creating or maintaining a culture, and we soon realized we'd been ignoring it for too long.

As the excitement over January's superb sales figures waned, veteran employees and new hires alike began to sense the irony: Culture was at the root of all of our success, but success was unraveling our culture. Our challenge: Hold on to one without giving up the other.

PART LOGIC, PART MAGIC

When you're doing culture really well, you don't notice you're doing it at all. Unlike the cleverly designed products bubbling out of our labs, there was no ingenious formula behind our culture. Like many successful start-ups, the shared values and behaviors that motivated us were largely a happy accident—the by-products formed when passionate, young, like-minded entrepreneurs defy industry expectations, change the world, and have fun in the process. Cool products, a clear vision, strong camaraderie, and a sense of purpose—virtually everything about the company was the result of smart, irreverent, devoted people doing everything in their own smart, irreverent, and devoted way.

Nowhere was this start-up serendipity more apparent than in our thriving and collaborative work atmosphere. It just took care of itself. When we hired a bright new employee, we did so because we instinctively felt he or she was the type of person we could imagine working alongside for ten, twelve, maybe sixteen hours a day. The Astroturf-lined Ping-Pong room? The cereal and beer in the office kitchen? These weren't contrived creature comforts cooked up during some HR workshop in the name of employee retention; they were the offbeat inspirations of earnest employees writing their own rules for the workplace. In short, we were benefiting from the paradox underlying all corporate cultures: Despite most companies' best efforts, the best cultures tend to be effortless.

So happy an accident was our culture, we didn't even have an HR depart-

▲ **THE ANNUAL METHOD PROM.** People rarely excel at anything unless they're having fun doing it.

ment devoted to maintaining it. Why should we? We owed much of our success to our willingness to shrug off the organizational theories and procedures that preoccupy MBA students and traditional administrators. Something so stiff and corporate-sounding as "human resources" just didn't belong in a rebellious, freewheeling upstart brand that held its own mock proms and organized itself into *pods* (our name for cross-functional product teams). Spontaneity and ingenuity, unfettered by bureaucratic process, were our lifeblood. Everyone's practical needs, from dental benefits to hang-ups with delegation, were handled on an ad hoc basis by a handful of the company's leaders, like the payroll coordinator, the controller, even our CEO. The result: an informal, collegial atmosphere based on common sense, honesty, mutual respect . . . and a lot of luck.

But after years of taking our culture for granted, rapid growth was wearing all of us down. Once second nature, our sense of identity and purpose flagged. At this point, an established company might have retraced its steps and made some minor adjustments, but we had nothing to adjust! We never had a plan for Method's culture. Since founding the company, it was all we could do to keep up with our growth. Six years later, everyone agreed that culture was our secret sauce . . . but no one had the recipe.

The culture problem was unlike any we had ever faced. This wasn't simply a matter of recalling a leaky valve or tweaking the ingredients in a new product. Identifying employees' concerns and formally establishing the brand's core values would involve some profound soul searching. In order to evolve, we had to regress, returning to a simple question with a profoundly complex answer: Who are we?

Despite our breakneck production schedule and our far-flung workforce—with ninety employees spread through three offices, in San Francisco, Chicago, and London—we made the decision that January to call an all-company offsite devoted to culture. Retreating to the California countryside with the entire staff, miles from the hustle and bustle of San Francisco and our crowded urban headquarters, we opened our minds, our notebooks, and the floor to our employees.

Some asked for better communication among the ever-growing number of pods. Others believed new employees needed more training in how to do things the Method way. Encouraged to speak freely, employee concerns ran the gamut. People wanted more career development and more feedback. They said they could have been on-boarded a little better or that we could be helping them become better recruiters. In essence, we'd been ignoring that stuff.

"Basically, people were asking for more structure, more process," says Anna Boyarsky, president of the Method Fan Club (aka advocacy director). "Process wasn't as necessary when we were smaller—our touch points were closer and the company was young and growing."

Culturally, there was very little *method* to Method—though we had always dismissed this irony with a grin and a shrug. But as concerns about preserving the company's culture mounted at our offsite, the atmosphere changed from levity to one of frustrated gravity. Listening to our employees' appeals, we began to appreciate a new irony. Afforded every freedom, our colleagues were requesting formality. Pardoned from protocol, they pleaded for procedure.

The idea of so much liberty in the workplace might be difficult for most people to imagine. Daydreaming in our cubicles between boardroom briefings with superiors and conference calls with subordinates, most of us long for a *less* regimented working environment. "If only we spent less time dealing with quarterly employee reviews, boring HR e-mails, and all those notorious TPS reports," we gripe, "maybe *then* we'd finally have some time to do our jobs!" Right. The swivel chair is always comfier on the other side of the cubicle partition. We forget that the same structure and process we malign is responsible for keeping everyone oriented, motivated, and accountable. We forget that, far from limiting creativity, structure and process often channel it in the right directions.

As crucial as spontaneity and ingenuity had been to our culture, the time had come to begin formalizing our approach. We began with notes about what mattered to our employees. Notebooks full of notes. Distilling everything down to a few core values was the challenge. And reintroducing these essential values—building them back into the day-to-day operations of the company—would come next. But how would we institutionalize Method's best practices without squeezing the life out of them and making the company feel like, well, an institution? The offsite was over, but as we barreled south toward the city on the 101 that rainy Sunday afternoon, all of us understood that the greatest journey our company would ever undertake—the quest to capture and preserve our culture—had only just begun.

THE QUEST TO DEFINE METHOD'S CULTURE

Like the age-old riddle about silence—which expires the moment you say its name—culture defies cultivation. The latest HR theories can no more measure a company's culture than an MRI can isolate an individual's soul. No drab mission statement ever inspired anyone to put in extra hours on a side project, no weekend team-building exercise in the forest ever got executives and hourly workers to sit side by side at lunch on Monday, and the world has yet to see an employee handbook capable of boosting employee morale. The greater the effort to formalize it—to box it in with structure and guidelines—the faster culture slips away. Nevertheless, diligent HR pros devote dense manuals full of prescriptive theory to its creation, only to throw up their hands, exasperated, when it materializes spontaneously in the ranks of unassuming start-ups all around them. At Method, we understood that too much process would only be an impediment. The challenge was to institute process without suffocating culture—but how?

"Our challenge as a company was, how do you keep the magic alive?" says Rudy Becker, the Resinator (aka engineering director). "It's one thing to succeed when you're small, but how do you keep all the good stuff while you grow? We knew what got us where we were and we didn't want to lose that. If we did lose it, it would almost not be worth it anymore."

In the midst of countless aimless discussions about how to fix Method's cul-

THE MINISTRY OF CULTURE

Imagine: An esteemed and empowered division of the company charged with maintaining a strong workplace culture that inspires employees, drives profits, and changes the world for the better. Some fantasy, right? Be that as it may, corporate America is forever forming subcommittees, executive councils, governing boards, special task forces, and ministries devoted to overseeing workplace culture. Most are distracting, grasping aimlessly with endless memos and pointless exercises (like the Ministry of Information in Terry Gilliam's *Brazil*). Others stifle the professional atmosphere with narrow guidelines and heavy-handed edicts (e.g., the Ministry of Truth in George Orwell's *1984*). But a rare few strike just the right balance, fostering the right conditions while still allowing things to take shape on their own.

Take a moment to identify the best aspects of your life at work and imagine how a group of devoted caretakers might help those aspects flourish. If you're still in the business-plan stage, make a list of all the qualities you envision in your ideal workplace and how you might encourage them on a day-to-day basis. Don't worry too much about what's practical at this stage—rather than an actionable plan, think of this as the ideal.

---

ture, our Big Spender (or CFO), Andrea Freedman, had an epiphany. What if we were to establish a pod to build and maintain our culture—a kind of ministry of culture?

The "Ministry of Culture" sounded great in theory, but we feared it would just be an HR department by another name. Furthermore, if culture was by definition greater than the sum of its parts, was it worthwhile—or even possible—to bother with the building blocks?

Questions like this got us thinking. More rules and guidelines were the wrong thing when the company was young and growing. We were small. Our touch points were closer. You didn't have to turn in a form for someone else to do something for you—you just walked over to the one person who did it. But as we grew and the company got bigger, we understood that some process might actually help free time and energy.

In search of how to introduce more process without smothering our culture, we consulted a handful of kindred spirits—companies we believe have built and maintained strong, organic cultures. After all, we've always been big believers in seeking inspiration from companies that do things better than we do—be it consumer-facing stuff like branding and packaging or behind-the-scenes areas of expertise like R&D and distribution. So, we figured, why not ask others' advice on culture?

In search of perspective, we approached six companies we knew and respected—Apple, Google, Pixar, Nike, Starbucks, and Innocent, the trendy British beverage maker—asking each of them one key question, "What really matters to you when it comes to great culture?" Unsurprisingly, the six had a lot to say. Taking it all down, we noticed three key themes common to all of them:

FOCUS ON HIRING GREAT PEOPLE Rather than hiring on expertise alone, make sure personalities and attitudes match your company. If you're about to hire someone and your gut tells you they're not a good fit, leave the seat open for now.

EMPHASIZE CULTURE FROM THE BEGINNING Explain the company's culture to new hires, making it clear to them that they were hired in part because of how they fit in.

GIVE PEOPLE LOTS OF FEEDBACK Take the time on a regular basis to remind your employees how they're doing vis-à-vis your values and culture.

In addition, we noticed that all our kindred spirits encouraged their employees to embrace a sense of purpose at work. It was less a rule than a value, a shared belief that motivated everyone in his or her unique way. Reflecting on our own situation, we understood that our culture needed a set of values that clarified our purpose as a company.

This was the turning point. Though we'd never before defined our values, Method had always been a purpose-driven company. Purpose was one of our key competitive advantages—motivating us to work harder, longer, and smarter than our competition. Shared values and purpose inspired us. There was only one thing left to do: articulate exactly what those were.

Combining our offsite notes with the suggestions we had gleaned from our culture idols, we recruited a handful of team members from various departments and asked them to work with our leadership team members to distill everything down to five core values. The team became known as the Values Pod.

Sure, we could have boiled everything down between the two of us, but we wanted our values to come from within. Years later, we discovered that companies like Zappos and Innocent had gone through the same process. (To say nothing of the founding fathers . . .) Consider the benefits. Drawing your values from the company ranks ensures that they will represent the richness of the brand, stay relevant at every level, and be embraced by employees year after year.

After incorporating input from every level of the company, our Values Pod presented us the final list:

Keep Method weird.
What would MacGyver do?
Innovate, don't imitate.
Collaborate, collaborate, collaborate.
Care like crazy.

Known collectively as our Methodology, these values have become the backbone of our culture obsession—a framework to provide our team members with direction and space to grow.

Our values help channel the frenetic atmosphere of innovation and quixotic spontaneity so vital to our success into a mutual sense of purpose. To integrate them into our day-to-day operations and make them actionable, we've printed them on cards illustrating how each value translates into behavior. By creating an annual deck of cards bound by a key ring, rather than a standard sheet of paper, people can hang the values at their desks, and they are easier to share. Along with the right physical reinforcements—like our open-office floor plan—our values cultivate the kind of environment that inspires the real magic: those everyday individual actions that make our company flourish.

Would our values work for you? Maybe. But adopting another company's values is like letting someone else design your dream house or write your wedding vows. Establishing your values is your chance to turn yourself inside out and see what you're really made of as a brand.

So, without further delay, here's a closer look at our Methodology.

KEEP METHOD WEIRD

Everyone knows what normal is. Normal is blue oxfords and khakis. Normal is a deck of PowerPoint slides. Normal is nine to five, taking your shoes off at the

▲ **WEIRD IS ABOUT SEEING THE WORLD DIFFERENTLY.** Let's face it, weird changes the world, and people remember weird.

door, and driving a Camry. Weird is everything normal is not. Weird is where you run into brilliant, independent, and risky. Weird can be inspiring, memorable, or outlandish. Weird is under no obligation to make sense.

Method is weird. We hope it shows in our products—the odd shapes, the unique fragrances, the quirky language sprinkled throughout our marketing and all over our packaging. Take one look around our office and it's clear the weirdness isn't just skin deep. From the random piñatas hanging from the ceiling (they tend to come and go around here) and the prom photos on the wall to the rock 'n' roll music in the elevator (it just made more sense than elevator music)—we do things differently.

We like the odd, offbeat, and outlandish so much, in fact, that we made "Keep Method weird" the first of our five values. To ensure we wouldn't turn into yet another big boring company full of boring people boring one another and our customers, we made sure to build weirdness right back into our formal rules, processes, and techniques. Yup, you heard it: Formality has a role in the fun.

We believe people don't perform at their highest levels unless they are having fun doing it. Ever notice when athletes are interviewed at the end of winning games, they typically mention how much fun they had? The same is true in business. If you can't be yourself at work, you're not going to do good work. This is especially important for us because we're trying to bring fun to an activity in which you rarely see it: cleaning.

That said, it's easy to interpret *weird* as simply having fun and doing strange stuff. (Like, say, keeping a secret stash of flamboyant hats—you never know when the right occasion might come about.) But it's important to leverage fun and use it to differentiate yourself in the marketplace. Having the courage to look at the world a little differently is what being weird is really about. And when you're competing against global, Goliath-size players, everything you do has to be different. Everyone who ever changed the world was considered weird at first, from Galileo to Gates.

WHAT WOULD MACGYVER DO?

At Method, Angus MacGyver* isn't just a source of inspiration—he's our mascot. Mac is the master of resourcefulness, a man who can turn a pencil, a rubber band, and a paperclip into a helicopter. Like us, Mac never had the same weapons as his nemeses, so he always had to be inventive and industrious to win a fight. If P&G has a fleet of F-16s, we have duct tape and a Swiss Army Knife.

▲ **TIPPING OUR HAT TO MAC.** MacGyver is our role model for resourcefulness.

---

* For those of you who missed the 1980s, please Google *MacGyver* . . . along with *The A-Team*, *Dallas*, and *The Love Boat*.

When we find ourselves facing a seemingly unsolvable problem, we ask ourselves, "What would MacGyver do?" This fresh perspective has served us well. No matter how large we grow, this value reminds us to embrace the scrappy attitude and creative irreverence that got us where we are. This value is about resourcefulness, knocking on the big door, and punching above your weight. After all, part of what has always defined us is our ability to outmaneuver major competitors despite having just a fraction of their manpower and infrastructure.

Finding our inner MacGyver means focusing on the solution, not the problem. Granted, this is a lesson we all learned in third grade, but somehow corporate America seems to forget it all the time. When you're a small company striving for growth, you have no choice but to figure out how to be resourceful with what you have to create solutions. When we didn't have marketing dollars, we just showed up in stores and performed demos. When Target's buyer declined our product line, we sent our pitch to the marketing department. Even with limited resources, there's always a way to win—just ask yourself, "What would MacGyver do?"

INNOVATE, DON'T IMITATE

Few terms in business are as overused or misused as *innovation*. The dictionary defines innovation as "the act of introducing something new." OK, but to us, innovation simply amounts to creativity applied to business—the process by which an organization generates creative ideas and converts them into useful products and services. The challenge is that process is about creating a predictable result, while innovation is about getting someplace new and unexpected. Using the first to get to the second is kind of like using a map to discover the New World—how do you chart a course to a place no one's ever been?

We believe the answer lies in creating an innovative culture in which new ideas can thrive. We try to foster an environment where we can expect the unexpected—be it our cross-functional pods, our open-to-all-ideas wiki walls, or our all-inclusive interview process. To do this, we try to think of everything as a beta test ("Ready! Fire! Aim!"). In practice, this translates into leveraging risk as a competitive advantage, routinely forgoing lengthy consumer testing trials, hastening internal development decisions, working with dynamic and flexible suppliers, and running parallel-track design efforts—just to see where all this leads us.

By now, you might be able to see how the values build on one another. If we have the courage to be weird and the resourcefulness of MacGyver, then innovation becomes that much easier.

COLLABORATE, COLLABORATE, COLLABORATE

The problem with growth is that it tends to separate people from one another, leaving them isolated from other groups. That's exactly what happened to us when we started to grow more quickly than we could manage. But in order to inspire collaboration, you have to break up silos and subcultures and improve cooperation, teamwork, and communication at every level of the company.

Collaboration is particularly important at Method because it's pivotal to our brand philosophy. Like all great brands, ours is built on inherent tensions—contrasting characteristics that don't typically go together. Tension is the wellspring of drama, spontaneity, innovation, energy, and culture. Think Target, combining low prices with high-end designers, or Starbucks, merging a brief daily escape with speedy convenience. Our mash-up: high design with environmental sustainability—two sensibilities generally at odds with each other.

Collaboration also operates on a granular level, factoring into everything we do. Without a general sense of goodwill (the assumption that everyone wants what's best for the company), every product launch would devolve into a battle. Few processes at Method demonstrate the goodwill we have for one another like the push and pull between our green chefs (our scientists) and our marketing department. While our green chefs want product labels to list every last environmental benefit (organic ingredients! no phthalates! packaged in 100% post-consumer bottles!), our marketers prefer to keep things simple (natural). Nevertheless, by assuming goodwill and understanding that we're all on the same team, we're able to work together to ensure the best outcome.

One of our favorite techniques for encouraging collaboration is the simple phrase "yes, and." Everybody knows the phrase "yes, but"—it's the reply our coworkers offer when they don't really agree with something we've just said. But a "yes, and" attitude turns this classic collaborative hang-up on its head. In fact, the "yes, and" attitude allows us to employ unconventional ideas like an open-office floor plan—one of the keys to the company's collaborative culture. Imagine trying to work alongside a colleague who's looking for the flaw in your thinking. A "yes, and" colleague is one who's willing to take your fragile idea and make it stronger. Give it a try next time you're brainstorming with a colleague. Rather than framing your response as an opposing idea, try starting with the words, "Yes, and . . ."

▲ SAYING "YES, AND . . ." When someone shares a new idea, don't discount it with a "yes, but." Instead, try "Yes, and . . ."*

Teamwork isn't about everyone thinking the same way; groupthink just creates a homogeneous—and stifling—culture. As mentioned, another way we create our culture is with our open and visual office-floor plan. For example, our green chefs are within shouting distance of our CEO, not in some windowless lab three states away, and our marketing, packaging, and creative specialists can share ideas and collaborate on everything from product stories and advertising to packaging and copyrighting without leaving their desks.

CARE LIKE CRAZY

Growth threatened to weaken our bonds, making it harder for individuals to identify the unique role they could play in the future of the company. If people didn't think their opinion mattered, they'd only be sticking around for a paycheck.

Like all of our values, care is about how we treat one another and how we treat everyone else, from consumers to retailers to the environment. If a colleague makes a contribution that nails one of our values, fellow team members can nominate that person for a values award. If a customer is anxious about how a product might affect her child, our customer-care specialists are there to field the call in person and answer every last question. Of course, "Care" has become something of a cliché when talking about corporate values, but let's be honest,

---

* This is an improv exercise which is all about accepting what others have to offer. When someone shares a new idea, don't discount something quickly with a "yes, but . . ." because it's something you've never encountered before. Instead, next time try starting your response with "yes, and . . ."

how many companies actually live up to this idea? You probably won't need two hands to count them.

Philanthropy is an important part of our care philosophy, which is why we give everyone on staff three paid days a year to help out a local cause (a program we call EcoManiacs). Naturally, employees are driven by different passions: Some have opted to support Moustache November (aka Movember), an effort to increase prostate cancer awareness in which participants either grow a mustache themselves or enlist others to do so. Others get behind Save the Bay, a wetlands restoration project in the San Francisco Bay Area in which employees have already cleaned up a nearby island.

Method employees adopt various causes but always from the same principle: Have a purpose greater than profits. As we see it, you spend so much of your life working, why not align your work with creating good? After all, people like having a job, but they especially like having a job that makes them feel good about themselves and their work. Whether we talk about laundry, wipes, or toilet-bowl cleaner, it all boils down to the same idea: How do we use our business to create positive change?

As a brand grows, employees tend to form cliques, leading to a breakdown in communication. If you want to care about someone, it helps to know them—yet so few companies put any effort into ensuring that employees know one another on a personal level throughout the company. So to keep everyone in touch, we launched a program called Reach-Out-First Lunches. Once every couple of months, we bring three baskets to the Monday huddle. We pick the name of a recent hire from the first basket, the name of an old-timer from the second basket, and the name of a restaurant from the third. The restaurants range from high-end steakhouses to the hot-dog stand up the street. Then we send the pair off to lunch with each other. The process encourages team members to care for one another like family—which, in a way, we are.

HOW WE LIVE OUR VALUES

Values are worthless unless you actually live them—in reality, most company values "live" on some dusty plaque, not in the soul of the brand. Who hasn't worked for a company that went to great lengths to define its values (offsites! surveys! consultants!) only to bury them in a handbook and refer to them sanctimoniously after someone really screwed up? That's HR and PR, not living your values. Values are what you practice when nobody—not even you—is paying attention.

A statement of our shared values and sense of purpose, our Methodology is the closest thing we have to a recipe for our culture. It's the logic that binds us together. When we get the logical parts just right, we create space for the magical, yielding amazing levels of collaboration and stellar business results. Swing by the San Francisco office sometime. We'll show you what we mean. But if you don't have time to say hi, here are a few examples of how we have learned to live our values every day.

HIRE RIGHT

Building weirdness into how you operate as a company isn't as difficult as it might sound—as long as you start at the beginning with whom you hire. The surest way to get a fast-growing company off track is to let the wrong people on the bus, as Jim Collins would say. Most companies fill open positions as quickly as possible for the sake of efficiency, but we would rather leave a job open for months than hire the wrong person. Case in point: Though our People and Environment Department (Method's answer to HR) was created in May 2008, we didn't hire a director until that November. Our colleagues even started referring to the vacancy as the Unicorn, because the right person for that position seemed as elusive as the mythical creature.

During our explosive growth years, we would hear things like "I just need a warm body to fill the seat," code for "We are about to compromise the talent level." No matter how you may rationalize it at the time, finding a warm body to fill the seat is *never* OK. Later in the book, we talk about "kicking ass at fast"— but when it comes to hiring, we like to take things slow by adding a number of speed bumps to the process that give us a chance to assess the applicant on a number of levels. Applicants may get all the way to the end of the process, but if no one stands out, we'll start it all over again with a new group.

Hiring at Method takes place in three stages: cross-functional interviewing, the homework assignment, and on-boarding. Our interview process employs a team of interviewers from around the company, so an applicant for a communications position might wind up discussing the job with an accountant, an industrial designer, a greenskeeper, and someone from our PR department. The message: You're joining an entire company, not just one department.

Yeah, seven or more interviews and a homework assignment is rigorous, and it's built up a reputation in the industry for being challenging. But we believe this is a good thing. After all, it communicates that we only want the

▲ THE LIVE AUDITION. Homework is our way of prototyping a relationship.

best, and it attracts talent with a high level of self-confidence. One benefit of the exhaustive process actually instills *greater* certainty: Better hiring means fewer firings.

One of the primary benefits of our interview process is that it allows the hire and the team to really get a sense of the chemistry. "I always ask, 'Is this a person that I'm excited to sit next to on a five-hour coast-to-coast plane ride?'" says Chief Person Against Dirty (or CEO, as some know him) Drew Fraser.

When we have a few candidates whom we love, we invite them back for our homework assignment. It's an integral part of our hiring process, and the first test is just watching their reaction. If they push back or aren't genuinely excited to give it a try, it's a major red flag. We once cut out of the running a CEO candidate who had previously led a billion-dollar consumer brand, because this person questioned the validity of doing homework. Yup, we're that serious about weird.

Every homework assignment consists of three questions: one strategic question, one tactical question—both customized for the applicant's experience—and then our favorite question: "How would you keep Method weird?" For example,

Don Frey, our Product Czar (aka vice president of product development), performed the Kermit the Frog song, "It's Not Easy Being Green" during his interview.

While it may sound like little more than a fun stunt, the homework assignment is actually a make-or-break rite of passage. It delivers a bounty of helpful insight, and we believe it's an excellent predictor of a candidate's success. It's a form of prototyping to see how candidates think and approach their work. It's a peek into their work ethic and a chemistry test for our culture. Matthew Loyd, our Brand Poobah (aka VP of brand experience), puts it this way: "You're in a room with ten or fifteen people. You're nervous, excited. It's pretty amazing what people come up with. One person Irish step-danced, someone took the staff out to do yoga in the lobby. Someone even made up a Method game show and passed out bells. She did a ton of research; she knew things many of us didn't know about the company!"

Some benefits of the homework assignment include:

It raises the bar for everyone. If you're the hiring manager and your candidate bombs in front of an audience, ultimately it makes you look bad. So everyone works harder at recruiting and screening top talent. The result is that it's harder for people to hire candidates weaker than themselves; because the process is so transparent, nothing slips by.

Bad talent can't hide in the homework. Sometimes the worst employees are the best interviewees just because they've done more interviews in their lives. (That, or maybe they're just really good bullshit artists.) With homework, you can get a better sense of how talented the candidates really are, allowing you to see how they think and problem-solve right in front of you.

Cash money. In some cases, homework assignments have saved us money because we were able to see that a less experienced, less expensive candidate actually had more talent. We always hire for talent over experience, and the homework assignment is the best way to distinguish between the two.

Due diligence. You can customize homework to a candidate's perceived or rumored weaknesses, allowing you to dig into any problem areas hinted at by interviews or reference checks.

Better sleep, all around. Hiring a new employee can be anxiety inducing for all involved, but homework removes most of that uncertainty. By the time they're finished working through the three-step homework assignment, new hires are already familiar with their colleagues and the company; they hit the ground running, making the first days and weeks much smoother.

Free ideas. Tons of them, actually. Homework provides the opportunity to learn from even the people you don't hire.

Scare the window-shoppers. Let's face it, a lot of people browse new jobs just to see if they can make more money. We keep them from wasting our time. You want an offer? You better be ready to work for it! In the end, this saves us a lot of time.

Silo Busting. Our unusual hiring process ensures that we hire unusual, dynamic people who are at ease outside their traditional comfort zone. These traits have become a pivotal part of what keeps us fresh. After all, once we find our unicorn, we change things regularly, looking for opportunities to move people around the company to broaden their experience. For example, a director may lead the laundry branch of the brand one year and transfer to personal care the next year. The process provokes employees to think creatively, spreading new strategies and lessons beyond traditional company silos.

A few years ago, we realized that while we were going to great lengths to get the right people on the bus, we were doing a lousy job of helping them make that transition. In response, we created a semiformal on-boarding approach.

On-boarding at Method starts on a Monday—everyone's first day—when they're introduced at the weekly all-company huddle (more on this below). When they're introduced, we ask them to share with everyone why they chose to join us and how they've pledged to keep Method weird. It's a great icebreaker and an energetic (and often humorous) start to everyone's first day. It's not uncommon to share embarrassing photos with the crowd (with the help of a conspiring spouse). From there, someone will walk them through our on-boarding book, our field guide to becoming a person against dirty. Highlights of the day include choosing your own title (we'll explain in a sec), rookie cookies (a plate of conversation bait that a new hire brings in to leave on the desk, no store-boughts allowed), and the presentation of an actual lotto ticket. That last part is a final check to ensure they're the right hire, not just born lucky.

As for titles, most companies just give you a title that defines your job and jurisdiction. In essence, you're labeled and put in a box. Fine if you just want people to do what's expected of them, but with fewer resources, we need every-one to punch above his or her weight. To empower our team members and give them a feeling of ownership, every new hire at Method gets to make up his or her own title. If you visit us, don't be surprised to meet a good cop (regulatory), a village voice (customer service), or a zookeeper (project manager). The process encourages independent thinking, confidence, and fun—and, perhaps most of all, it emphasizes how every person at the company has an important role in driv-ing change.

While new hires will always change an established culture to some degree, they bring an infectious curiosity and energy to the mix. By taking the effort to instruct them and fully integrate them into the company, existing employees can harness that energy themselves.

MONDAY MORNING HUDDLES

The Monday morning huddle is an informal gathering in our front lobby where we share information and employees have an opportunity to share concerns and personal news. (To give credit where credit is due, we admit we stole this idea

▲ **HUDDLE UP!** Our caffeinated kick start to the week that keeps everyone connected to the culture.

from Richard Reed, cofounder of Innocent. Thanks, Richard!) At Method, the huddle is our way of aligning our obsessions with our objectives and keeping the company on track. New contracts, financial challenges, birthdays of the week, a reminder to do the dishes—each huddle is dedicated to discussing and preserving everything that makes us who we are as a company.

If you've never done it, the Monday morning huddle may sound awkward or plain unnecessary, but it's a great example of where logic and magic have intersected for us. Employees asked us for more structure and process at work (the logic half), so we decided to devote time to discussing shared goals, challenges, insights, and solutions (the magic half). We also hand out values awards—one of

HOLD A MIRROR TO IT

Every six months, we run a "come clean" survey that measures how everyone is feeling about the culture and their respective roles. Typical statements (scored 1 to 5) might include, "I look forward to coming to work every day," "I believe Method will do great things," and "I have a positive relationship with my boss." Afterward, we hold everyone accountable for improving the scores by updating the results at one of our Monday morning huddles. When something feels off—a negative comment about poor collaboration in a particular department, say, or an antagonistic question about promotion opportunities (or lack thereof), we address it by "holding a mirror to it." To do this, we put the note up on a slide (removing the author's name, of course) and, rather than answer it ourselves, open it up to our team members for discussion. The process helps clear the air and reinforces the idea that everyone is accountable to the success of our culture.

Mirroring is a good barometer for where things stand because it forces people to ask, "Who do we want to be as a company—and who's going to be responsible for that?" No matter who you are, with culture, the answer is always "me." At one of our offsites, we got a note that said something like, "The culture at Method is broken, what is the leadership of this company going to do about it?" We mirrored it, and our colleagues were visibly shaken up. It got people thinking, and the response was like an organ rejection. "Why would someone say that?" they asked. "Culture is *everyone's* responsibility."

the bottom-up ways fellow team members can recognize one another for doing great work and one of the most overt ways we live our values. In order to nominate someone for a values award, team members submit a short story about what their colleague did and how it lived up to one of our values. If approved, the recipient gets a chance to spin a wheel and win fabulous prizes, from a frozen turkey to lunch with one of our packaging engineers. Yes, all very fabulous . . . and weird.

How much do we love our weekly huddle? We specifically designed our lobby for it, complete with funky couches and a killer A/V system. To be clear, a weekly staff meeting in the company boardroom is not a huddle, it's a staff meeting. Hold your huddle somewhere informal—the lobby, the kitchen, that back hallway with the old Xerox machine and the drafty skylight—anywhere but a conference room.

Another way we distinguish the huddle from an everyday meeting is by assigning a different person to "take point" each week. Though the main agenda is always the same—examining our priorities by way of our seven obsessions—changing the moderator helps everyone see each obsession from a fresh perspective. Take the first obsession, culture. Handled with a bit of personality, such as a Big Lebowski theme—complete with cereal bowls, shabby bathrobes, and gratuitous use of the word *dude*—even simple announcements about birthdays, personal milestones, and weekly front-desk assignments take on a new dimension. To start off the huddle, each week's leader will read a letter from one of our advocates (the name we give our customers) reminding us whom we really work for—them.

Next Monday, try a huddle with your company or your department. It may feel odd at first, but as you settle into a groove, it becomes an authentic way of reinforcing your shared values, aligning everyone toward company goals, and simply kicking off the week.

CORN DOGS AND PROM QUEENS

Like the weekly huddles, company events reinforce our values. Both of our annual company offsites are largely devoted to discussing and sharing the values. This may take the form of town-hall conversations about recent challenges, reviewing the Come Clean survey results, or an exercise in which we ask people to break up into groups and tackle a tough, open-ended question like "What would it look like if our culture were our number-one competitive advantage?" In addition, each summer's prom—yes, there is a prom committee and a new prom theme

▲ **BRANDING FROM THE INSIDE OUT.** At Method the employees are the brand.

every year (recent themes include "Under the Sea" and "Heroes and Villains")—is dedicated to celebrating our values. Regardless of the event in question, costumes generally come into play. At one event, we gave everyone in the company a cape, because, well, everybody sounds smarter wearing a cape. (Try it sometime.) On the surface, proms and costumes in a professional environment may sound weird . . . and they are! But when some of your employees work eight thousand miles apart and only see one another a couple times a year, irreverent touches like this break down social walls and provide something creative and entertaining to bond over. To collaborate well on the hard stuff, we need everyone to know and feel comfortable with one another.

We encourage everyone to come up with ideas for events, funding and promoting them whenever possible. This can mean everything from a ski trip or a rotating drink cart to Corndog Appreciation Day. Not to be outdone, every March 14 (3/14) the finance department celebrates the number pi (π) by baking pies with decimals etched into the crust. Whether it comes from the top down or the bottom up, fun and weirdness are contagious.

DON'T START A BUSINESS, START A CAUSE

After ten years in business and hundreds of innovations, we can still confidently say that our proudest achievement remains our first—launching a company with a social mission to do good in the world by giving people a great, healthy, cool product that is good for them and the environment. Not only was creating a mission-driven company the right thing to do for society and the planet; we've proven that it's the right thing to do for the bottom line, too. The rapid expansion of media transparency is producing increasingly well-informed and discriminating consumers. The influx of socially and environmentally conscious Gen Y-ers into the workforce is redefining the war for talent. Challenges to the most established businesses, these shifts present significant competitive advantages to mission-driven companies.

Beyond the profound public impact this mission has had throughout our industry, our community, and our environment, the cultural advantage of having a purpose larger than profits has been key to the adoption and application of our values. Most corporate values are just that—the values of the corporation. No matter how much ambition, camaraderie, and loyalty an employee brings to work, no one is taking those corporate values home to share with friends and family. But those same values become immeasurably more meaningful when they're tied to a higher purpose.

On an individual level, our team members are passionate about our values because they know they're making a difference in the world. It's human nature to want to be a part of something bigger than oneself. We are amazed at how many cover letters we get that open with lines like, "My goal is to work for a values- and mission-driven business." If people don't love what they are doing or feel that they're a part of something important, they'll go somewhere else.

Of course, working with purpose and values isn't just a matter of individual growth; finding meaning in work is central to a strong corporate culture. In fact, the power of sharing our values collectively far exceeds any individual benefit. Even when we don't follow the same passions, we are united by the fact that we are all committed to a greater cause. Working for the common good helps us put ego aside and work collaboratively as a team, engendering a deep sense of continuity, familiarity, and trust that spills over into every discipline in the company.

Building a shared vision around a social mission takes a different leadership style than most of us are accustomed to. At Method, this means never forgetting that money isn't what primarily motivates our colleagues. Like us, they're driven by making the world a cleaner place. We know this because they tell us as much at group offsites, in community volunteer efforts, and over drinks after work. Good leaders encourage this kind of passion in their employees. Great leaders leverage it and channel it, outrecruiting and outperforming their soulless corporate rivals.

ERROR AUTOPSY: MACGYVER'S BETRAYAL

Perhaps it was inevitable that a guiding principle intended to inspire ingenuity would ultimately become an excuse for cutting corners. But MacGyver taught us that living by your values isn't always as clear as it sounds and can quickly turn into MacGruber, the *Saturday Night Live* parody. We started spotting the warning signs early on . . .

At every Monday's weekly huddle, team members can nominate any colleague for a values award. In the beginning, praise poured in, the prize wheel spun, and all was well with the world. That is, until we noticed a growing pattern: Someone would get hung up on a project, pull an all-nighter, air-freight the finished product at the last possible second, and barely meet the deadline. "Success!" Afterward, everyone would let out a huge sigh of relief, and the next day the employee would be nominated for a MacGyver award! OK, but . . .

Examples like this were why What Would MacGyver Do? quickly became our most common award. People would screw around, pull something out of their ass at the last minute, then sit back and bask in the limelight. As leaders, we had to help our team members to stop MacGyvering on the back end and start doing more work on the front end. MacGyver didn't merely divert the enemy, defuse the bomb, and devise an escape route, all at the last second. He applied the same assiduous insight from the opening scene through the whole episode. Sure, maybe savvy TV producers made sure all the important plot twists were served up in the last two minutes, but MacGyver wasn't asleep during the first fifty-eight.

The point is, just because your values are well intentioned doesn't mean they can't be manipulated or lead people astray. When that happens (and it will, trust us), it's up to leadership to step in and set things straight.

▲ ZAPPOS CULTURE BOOKS. Every year Tony asks employees to write, "What does Zappos culture mean to you?" Except for correcting typos, they leave it unedited and publish everything in a book available to anyone, which creates both transparency and accountability for their culture.

OUR CULTURE MUSE: TONY HSIEH, CEO OF ZAPPOS

When it comes to great culture, we have a lot of muses, but the person we have stolen from more than anyone else is Tony Hsieh, the CEO of Zappos. As an entrepreneur, Tony is a tough act to follow. He has hit two home runs and recently took Zappos to a billion-dollar acquisition by Amazon.com. (And Tony's first book, *Delivering Happiness,* hit number one on the *New York Times* bestseller list, another accomplishment we'd like to emulate.) We met Tony briefly a few times in San Francisco and even attended one of his epic loft parties. But it wasn't until we were summoned to the White House with a group of entrepreneurs in 2008 that we had the opportunity to bond with him. In Tony Hsieh we found a kindred spirit for culture, mission-driven business, and the occasional tequila shot. OK, maybe more than occasional.

If you've read Tony's book, you might think we stole his "weird" value . . . in fact, he and we both came up with that one on our own. Weird coincidence, huh? No matter whether you come to it independently or steal it from us, weirdness is a great value for a creative business.

AT METHOD, WE DON'T
HAVE RECEPTIONISTS.

everyone gets a chance to moonlight
up front, which, we hope, explains any
incompetence you might encounter,
not that you will.

method

▲ **MAY WE HELP YOU?** When everyone has "receptionist" in their job title, it's tough to have a big ego.

In fact, after a tour of Zappos, our leadership team took one of Tony's great ideas—doubling the reception desk to feature two people, making a more engaging, social impression—and made it even weirder, replacing our receptionist with the Method House of Representatives. Each day, two different Method team members work the front desk. The change helps us maintain the small-company feel, reinforce community, and keep the ego out of the ranks. Trust us: There's nothing more delightful than seeing the CEO deliver the office mail!

After establishing the habit, it wasn't long before the rotating House of Representatives started declaring a new theme each day. Swing by our office sometime and you might be offered a shot of Jägermeister by an overly tanned host (*Jersey Shore* Day) or find yourself face-to-face with a Billy Idol look-alike (Punk Rock Day).

Weird? Absolutely! Fun? You know it! Scalable? We get asked that a lot, actually, and it's an important question. As we've discovered, maintaining your culture as you grow is one of the hardest things to do in business. But thanks in part to the example set by Tony and Zappos (with three thousand employees and $1 billion in sales and growing), we're confident that you don't have to be small to be weird. See you in Vegas, Tony!

obsession

2

INSPIRE
ADVOCATES

don't sell to customers,
create advocates for
your social mission

CAN YOU RECALL THE LAST ADVERTISEMENT YOU saw? We're not talking about the most memorable—the good ads that made you laugh or got you thinking, or one of the viral spots you forwarded to your friends via e-mail or on Facebook. No, we're speaking literally here: the very last commercial that flashed across the screen before you turned off the TV last night, the final billboard you zoomed by on the way home from work, that pesky pop-up ad lurking behind your browser when you logged off the computer earlier.

Drawing a blank?

We can't remember either. After encountering an estimated five thousand ads a day, who can? Each year, U.S. businesses spend more than $300 billion on paid media—TV, print, online, et cetera—in an increasingly desperate effort to capture our attention. Amid the ten-grand-a-second barrage, most of the ads we see (or don't see, as it turns out) pass by unnoticed. For those particularly persistent spots, we now have our choice of a growing number of ad-blocking technologies and ad-free services. DVRs, spam filters, satellite radio, podcasts, the National Do Not Call Registry—as long as advertisers keep inventing new ways to interrupt us, industrious entrepreneurs will devise new ways to block them.

While all this ad-free media and technology is great news for consumers, it presents an intimidating challenge for consumer brands like us and probably your company too. Imagine launching a new brand in a multibillion-dollar consumer packaged goods category like ours. You've got Procter & Gamble—the biggest advertiser on earth, which in 2010 spent $4.2 billion on advertising in the

United States alone. Unilever spent another $1.3 billion. It's safe to assume these guys have a toilet-paper budget that's bigger than our entire marketing budget (even accounting for the fact that they *make* toilet paper and get it at cost).

In contrast, Method didn't even have a dollar to spend at launch. Our marketing strategy consisted of spending money on better packaging and doing personal demos in grocery stores. Not that we let the ad-spending disparity get to us; long before our first products reached shelves, we knew we'd have to come up with our own creative alternatives to traditional advertising in order to reach potential customers. Besides, even if we'd had a million bucks for marketing, it would have amounted to just one three hundred–thousandth of the overall ad market's annual commercial cacophony. Our message and our money would have been lost in an instant. Ten years later, not much has changed: The easiest thing to hide in America is a million dollars of advertising.

THE BIG SHIFT: GOING FROM PAID TO EARNED MEDIA

The problem with paid media isn't the content. Some of those advertising billions actually result in fun, creative, insightful campaigns. The problem is the context—how it's served up and how we consume it. If the gloomy ad-industry stories filling the business pages of our newspapers and magazines weren't evidence enough of the dwindling influence and relevancy of mass advertising, the fact that we've stopped flipping through those very pages in favor of clicking through them (opting out and blocking pop-ups as we go) is a fitting reminder. Media is changing. The "golden era" of mass advertising—the fabled *Mad Men* days when one thirty-second toothpaste commercial during the nightly news reached a vast swath of U.S. consumers—is dead and gone.

The spread of on-demand cable television, the Internet, and various other new ways to consume media—from the Kindle to the iPad—has revolutionized how we shop and share opinions. Modern consumers no longer sit around in front of the television waiting for Don Draper to tell them why they should buy Cocoa Puffs and Colgate. Today, we choose the brands we want to interact with, and we block out the rest. As consumers, we no longer want to be a passive audience; we want to be participants. It's a sea change in how consumers shop and how brands do business. We call it the *big shift*.

Few of the opportunities we discuss in this book present as many advantages to the next generation of entrepreneurs as the big shift from paid media to earned media. We consider *paid media* any form of marketing that requires you to pay a fee for the privilege of interrupting a predictable number of consumers ("please excuse the commercial interruption"). These include the billboard on I-5 that interrupted your morning commute, the television ad that you fast-forwarded through while enjoying the eightieth season of *The Bachelor* last night, and the print ad in *US Weekly* right next to "Stars, They're Just like Us!" In contrast, *earned media* are any media your company receives for free, including press hits, social media, blog posts, or viral videos on YouTube. Even this book is earned media for us because we didn't pay you to read it. Well, at least we hope not. In each case, the media are earned by creating something that people actually want to share or participate with.

Previous media shifts—newspapers to radio, radio to television—were simply transitions from one form of paid interruption media to another. Even when the medium changed, the biggest advertisers still held on to the advantage. But emerging social and earned media distinctly favor young, fast-moving businesses over their older, slower rivals. Ten years ago, when Method was just getting off the ground, few people had ever heard of a blog, let alone social media. Twitter and Facebook didn't exist yet. Today, new tools offer challenger brands better ways to market on a budget, find their place in a crowded industry, and earn more meaningful press and word of mouth—all for free. So why are companies still pumping $300 billion a year into paid media when earned media is free and consumers are doing everything in their power to ignore, erase, filter, or block them out? If they're the masters of messaging, you'd think they would get the message: Don't call us, we'll call you.

Most companies continue to buy traditional advertising for the same reasons nearly all of us continue to use fossil fuels: Making such a profound shift in our way of life is incredibly difficult. Systemwide change is expensive, disruptive, and time-consuming. And leveraging all the new tools at your disposal isn't going to be easy. Right now we are only partway through the shift, so it's a very awkward time in history to be a marketer. And it's about to get really hard. While the old media tools are quickly becoming less efficient, they still often represent the best way to reach a mass audience with a high level of predictability. Even though we are dedicated to the emerging powers of earned media, Method will spend a record level on advertising this year to boost awareness of our brand. We are stuck between the two media worlds, so the only way to navigate this transition is make sure that any form of paid media works hard to create an earned-media halo. Few have nailed this as well in the recent past than those who relaunched Old Spice in 2010. What began as a few million dollars in paid

▲ **INVITING A DIALOGUE.** Our crowd-sourced music video invites participation so advocates help us build the brand.

advertising resulted in an immeasurable amount of earned media in months of YouTube, TV, print, and online coverage, turning Isaiah Mustafa into a cultural icon. The genius of the campaign was that it spoke directly to both men and women and generated a conversation about body wash. Once the campaign was established through paid media, Old Spice gave consumers an opportunity to participate directly with a "response" campaign wherein fans and celebrities could contact Isaiah directly—and receive a video response from him in real time! Ultimately, earned media overshadowed paid media, but it took the balance of both to create such a big impact.

While the big shift may look like just a media shift, the impact on brand building is much more profound. The brands that rose to power in the last fifty years were fueled by mass media. They didn't succeed by spending the most on mass media; they succeeded because they efficiently aligned their brand and organizational structure around a mass-media approach. The key to this formula was targeting the largest group of people and positioning the brand upon its broadest and simplest attribute—the lowest common denominator that appealed to the largest number of people. But as mass media disappears, so do mass brands.

See the pattern here? Brands have always lived and died amid changes in consumer media consumption, and the shift to social media is no different. As old media platforms continue to sink, brands unable to make the leap will drown. Nevertheless, most companies are rearranging deck chairs on the *Titanic*, refusing to see that brands built on single-attribute messaging and broad relevance have little appeal in an era of infinitely fragmented, socially driven media. Of course, the idea behind social and earned media isn't new—word of mouth has been around since the first caveman told his friend where to hunt the best woolly mammoth. The difference is that this shift dramatically amplifies word of mouth; instead of one mom telling her ten closest friends about one of your products, she has the power to share her perspective about your brand with millions of other moms all over the world in seconds.

What's particularly different about this shift is that it moves the advantage from the companies with the most ad dollars to companies with the most compelling mission. People may see and remember an ad, but they will spread and bond over a great mission, thus allowing your idea to spread further than your marketing budget could take you.

Thus, to succeed in a world of earned and social media requires you to shift your mind-set from talking to customers to inspiring advocates, which is Method's second obsession. What's an advocate? As we see it, advocates are more than just consumers; advocates are evangelists for your brand. The dictionary defines an advocate as "a person who publicly supports or recommends a particular cause or policy." The ability to create advocates is the most important prerequisite for a brand championing social change and challenging the establishment. Not only do advocates make good business sense by buying more of our products more often, but also they engage us—online, in writing, on the phone, and in person—teaching us all sorts of stuff we wouldn't have figured out on our own. This kind of feedback is more honest, more complete, and a lot faster than that of our casual consumers, enabling us to be more innovative. *Advocate* is more than just a fancy word for customer. As we see it, calling our best customers advocates reframes how we think of them and in turn how we serve them.

Besides engaging us directly, advocates engage others, helping to spread our message. Whether it's talking about us to their friends and family, reviewing our products online, or forwarding our most recent viral spot, the best way to recruit new advocates is through existing advocates. Take Nathan Aaron, one of our biggest online advocates and the man behind Methodlust.com. Few rock bands or movie stars have as devoted a fan as Nathan. An illustrator and graphic designer from Greensboro, North Carolina, Nathan has been blogging about Method for years. Nathan doesn't blog once a month or every week; he writes almost daily, posting even more than we do on our own blog. Having recognized the value of such a voice, Method has nurtured Nathan's lust by responding to requests for interviews, sending updates on Method products, and supplying Nathan with pictures and other content.

Among the many features on Nathan's fan site are links to new product releases, retired products, video reviews, contests, reader polls ("What's your favorite Method line?" "Which new scent should Method pick?"), and even alter-

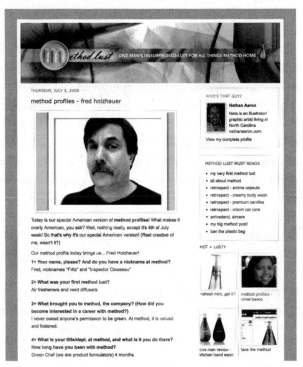

▲ **FRIENDS WITH BENEFITS.** As a fan of the brand, Nathan's blog methodlust.com helps spread our mission and keeps us honest.

native uses for Method products—such as lamps made from our dish-soap bottles and shower spray used as bug repellent. While much of this comes from his readers, Nathan maintains close contact with Method itself, a connection that enables him to break news about the brand, link to Method's various Twitter feeds, and present some two dozen exclusive profiles and interviews—photos included—of Method employees at every level of the company.

Despite his odes to limited-edition scents and his open declaration of desire (literally: "This blog is one man's unsuppressed lust for Method home products"), Nathan is not afraid to sound off on the brand he loves. When a product fails to live up to his high standards (or those of his readers), he'll offer a detailed breakdown of how it might be improved. And when products don't appear as anticipated, he'll speak his mind: "Method, we WANT our holiday aroma pills and sprays next year! This is a threat, I repeat, a threat! Are you all with me, Method lusters! Let's start a Method-olution!" A helpful ally, and, occasionally, a loving adversary, Nathan represents the ideal brand advocate.

The idea of creating advocates like Nathan (whom we love), who want a higher level of participation with a brand, is not new. After all, weekend warriors were getting Harley-Davidson tattoos long before we were born. What we brought to the party was proof that you can build advocacy around a low-interest category and use the new powers of earned media to effectively compete against the world's largest advertisers in mass categories. But turning your marketing on its head to inspire advocates demands turning a lot of other things upside down, too, like how you run your business and how you serve your customers. Once you've done the heavy lifting, however, the results will take on a life of their own. Your beliefs and your behaviors will do your marketing for you, your employees and advocates will promote your brand on your behalf, and your competitors will be left to find a niche of their own. To get there, we built our brand around a set of beliefs, branded from the inside out, and invited participation. Here is our Method method for inspiring advocates.

START WITH A BELIEF

The difference between a mass-market brand and a belief brand is like the difference between a monologue and a dialogue. Mass brands talk at people. Or more accurately, they SHOUT! Belief brands, on the other hand, listen and create a conversation. And if you ask us, the world could use fewer of the former and more of the latter. As it is, however, most modern brands don't have the social skills to invite a dialogue with their consumers because doing so requires great listening skills which is really hard for most marketers. That's because most of today's brands are promise-based brands ("always low prices"), not philosophy-based brands (help you live better). But brand relationships are like human relationships; if they're based on a promise—a one-sided idea—there's no depth to the relationship. The result is that many existing brands built in the mass-media era offer little for consumers to bond over.

In contrast, a brand philosophy is subtler, more complex. Not only does a philosophy take more time to communicate than a promise, but the appropriate audience is also much smaller. That's because your beliefs and values need to resonate with your audience before they become *shared* beliefs and values. Until recently, this wasn't easy—especially for start-ups trying to get a toehold in an established market. Promises and philosophies had to go head-to-head in mass advertising, competing with repetition, volume, and variety. In the race to the bottom, every company had to streamline its message, paring away personality and depth. But the arrival of social media means philosophy-based brands have more ways to express themselves and tell a deeper story, inviting people to discover every special detail on their own time rather than interrupting them with some reductive promise.

Not only is social media well suited to philosophy-based brands, but the social shift is making it harder for promise brands to get away with the same old tricks. With a few exceptions—like promising the lowest price—consumers are less and less satisfied with simple brand promises. We want brands that engage us, brands that show us a richer world. Look no further than Gen Y. Their formative years were during the prosperous late 1990s. Amid the abundance, the consumer question for a brand was, "Who are you and what can you offer?" This represented a shift from not just what consumers buy but what they *buy into*.

With so much to choose from, Gen Y's purchasing decisions became based on shared values. As a result, they're choosier and more social, interactive, and curious than any generation before them. They ask more of the brands they love. And increasingly they're calling the shots, purchasing a greater and greater percentage of goods versus preceding generations. Brands with personality, such as Lush, Ben & Jerry's, or Innocent also demonstrate consumer resistance to homogenization. Driven by our senses toward what is real and authentic, we prefer the character of a boutique market over a sterile strip mall, and character is difficult for big brands to achieve on a mass scale. We wholeheartedly believe that mission- or values-driven brands will be the brands of the future.

In building a belief brand, a company has to tap into what we call its social

method.humanifesto

as people against dirty,

we look at the world through bright-green colored glasses.

we see ingredients that come from plants, not chemical plants.

we see that guinea pigs are never used as guinea pigs.

we're entranced by shiny objects like clean dinner plates, floors you could eat off of, nobel peace prizes, and tasteful public sculptures.

we're an e.o.m.e.d. (equal opportunity movement for environment and design). method is our way of keeping the movement, well, moving.

we make role models in bottles.

we're the kind of people who've figured out that once you clean your home, a mess of other problems seem to disappear too.

we always see the aroma pill as half full, and assume everyone we meet smells like fresh-cut grass or a similar yummy nothing-but-good fragrance.

we exercise by running through the legs of the giant.

and while we love a freshly detoxed home, we think perfect is boring, and weirdliness is next to godliness.

it's "everybody into the pool!"(we believe in spontaneous bursts of enthusiasm.)

we also believe in making products safe for every surface, especially earth's.

we consider mistakes little messes we can learn from—nothing that can't be cleaned up and made better.

we embrace the golden ylang-ylang rule: do unto your home as you would do unto you. (your shower doesn't want to have morning breath any more than you do.)

we believe above all else that dirty, in all its slime, smoggy, toxic, disgusting incarnations is public enemy number one.

good always prevails over stinky.

▲ **OUR HUMANIFESTO.** What statement about humanity does your brand make?

mission. Consumers are much more likely to participate and share your brand with others if they can get behind you and what you stand for, rather than just the products you deliver. At Method, we started a movement to get "dirty" out of people's homes. A movement to protect the planet while cleaning it up. And a movement to show that business can be an agent of social change. As People Against Dirty, we come to work every day to try to make the world a cleaner and healthier place. For us, People Against Dirty will always be more than a tagline. Not sure you have a social mission? Don't worry. This is one of those things that sounds more high-minded than it really is. Any brand has the potential to have a social mission even if it doesn't necessarily translate to the greater good of society. Take Axe body spray, for example. Axe's social mission: helping young men get laid. Granted, it may not be noble, but it's one hell of a social mission! Consider a few others:

Method (us!), inspire a happy healthy home revolution	▶	People Against Dirty
TOMS Shoes, the socially conscious footwear brand	▶	Make Life More Comfortable
Kashi, the natural foods company	▶	Seven Whole Grains on a Mission
Zappos, the online retailer famous for great customerXW service	▶	Delivering Happiness
Nike, the iconic sports brand	▶	Just Do It

A social mission is important because, for human beings, a critical attribute of happiness is the ability to be part of something bigger than ourselves. We crave meaning in our lives and careers. As we pointed out in chapter 1 while discussing our obsession with culture, building a brand around a social mission energizes our entire organization and motivates us every day to make the world a better place. It transforms a career into a calling. Better yet, among advocates, this passion is contagious if you can present a world that they want to see too. But to do it well, you have to build a brand from the inside out.

BUILDING A BELIEF BRAND

We admit it: We were never passionate about cleaning before we launched Method. But building a belief brand with a social mission taught us that there is no such thing as a low-interest category, just low-interest brands. Anyone can generate excitement about a new cell phone technology or a new beer brand. Attracting attention in a traditionally low-interest category (like soap) takes a bit more thought. This is one of the best benefits of belief brands—they work equally well in crowded high-interest categories and in overlooked categories. Beyond the emotional engagement created by sharing similar beliefs and values with their advocates, belief brands have a philosophy, an attitude, and a story to tell. Their personalities aren't created in some office on Madison Avenue; they're woven into the very fabric of the organization. Below, a few examples of high-interest brands in low-interest categories:

> **Joe Boxer.** By injecting irreverence and controversy into his Joe Boxer brand, Nicholas Graham transformed everyday boxer briefs into a conversation piece.

> **Dyson.** Ten years ago, it would have been difficult to imagine anyone getting excited about a vacuum cleaner. Dyson shook up the dusty category with innovative technology and beautiful design.

> **Swingline.** An unremarkable and ubiquitous tool, staplers were the poster boy of low interest before Mike Judd cast a red Swingline as an object of devotion in his 1999 corporate satire *Office Space*.

While we rely primarily on style and substance to inspire interest in cleaning products, we also tap into an often overlooked subset of consumers: people who actually love to clean. You probably even know a few friends whom you consider to be clean freaks. We believe in making the act of cleaning more enjoyable and, if we may say so, aspirational. But virtually every commercial treats cleaning as if it were a huge hassle, virtually screaming promises of convenience and ease. Pandering to women with images of grinning maids in aprons, it was as if taking care of your things was something to be ashamed of, something you'd rather leave to someone else. This is typical problem-solution marketing, in which you set up a problem (mildew in the bathroom) and then present your product as the hero solution (*Pow!* mildew gone). The problem with this approach is that it forces the consumer to enter through the problem, so your brand will always live in low-interest land. Even if you don't find an ounce of joy in cleaning, virtually everyone loves the end state, a clean home. So we focused on talking about the aspirational end state of cleaning, and we found that, to many people, cleaning is an important part of life. It's the ritual of connecting to their homes and families by putting life back in order. To many, cleaning is a form of caring for their children or pets by providing a safe haven for those they care about most.

Seeking to draw out our audience's inner clean freaks, we filled our ad campaigns with young, great-looking naked people in gorgeous, hip homes, using (or maybe just caressing) a rainbow of beautiful Method products. Rather than the "quick and painless" promises in our competitors' ads, we communicated

▲ **DETOX POP SHOP.** Inviting advocates to turn in their toxic cleaners.

with clever, cheeky messages intended to promote the aspirational idea that cleaning could be cool (*gasp!*). Flying in the face of decades of traditional cleaning commercials, the ads resonated with people of all ages.

To many people, jogging is a chore. Imagine if Nike ran advertisements featuring unhappy joggers forcing themselves through another grueling early morning routine. Not likely. To the contrary, the brand celebrates every sport it touches, with aspirational imagery. We'd even bet there are some fierce badminton ads out there that would inspire you to Just Do It with a birdie! Nike ties this to its social mission of bringing inspiration and innovation to every athlete in the world. As Bill Bowerman, track coach and cofounder of Nike, said, "If you have a body, you are an athlete."

Bottom line: If you're struggling to shift your brand from low to high interest, seek to reframe your communications from presenting the problem to projecting the desired end state and wrap that in a social mission.

BRAND FROM THE INSIDE OUT

While most companies treat marketing as an external activity—something that focuses on spreading a message outside the walls of your company—the truth is that building a belief brand starts on the inside. In this new transparent media environment, your employees are your brand, and everything that goes on inside your walls can be shared with the outside world. If not for the Internet, brand horror stories, like the one about the Domino's employee spitting into food, would be just urban legends. But thanks to the Web, we can share brands' most embarrassing moments with the world—Steven Slater's infamous resignation as a JetBlue flight attendant or all those Comcast repairmen caught sleeping on people's couches. See what we mean when we say your employees are the brand?

It's been said that you can't learn the game as a spectator—you need to play it. We couldn't agree more. Building a brand starts with you, and at Method, we're dedicated to creating the kind of products we'd want our families to use, and we hire passionate people who resemble our consumers. Believe it or not, this approach is actually counterintuitive for most big brands; they like to keep a healthy distance between their employees and their consumers to ensure "an objective point of view." Maybe this worked in the past, but in an era defined by social media—where our personal and professional lives are increasingly melded and public—this kind of thinking is flawed at best.

At Method, we *want* to blur the lines between who we are and whom we serve. We are proud to be our own advocates. After all, why would we want to sell something we didn't love ourselves? If you walk into our office and meet our team, they should remind you of our brand. If you sit next to someone on a flight who works at Method, you should expect to meet an optimistic, fun individual who cares deeply about the environment and might even buy you a drink. We

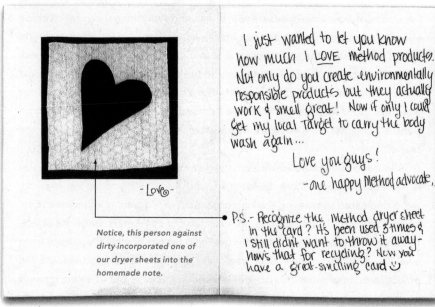

I just wanted to let you know how much I LOVE method products. Not only do you create environmentally responsible products but they actually work & smell great! Now if only I could get my local Target to carry the body wash again...

Love you guys!

-one happy method advocate,

- Love -

Notice, this person against dirty incorporated one of our dryer sheets into the homemade note.

P.S.- Recognize the method dryer sheet in the card? It's been used 5 times & I still didn't want to throw it away - how's that for recycling? Now you have a great-smelling card ☺

▲ **FAN MAIL.** In today's marketing environment, listening is more important than talking.

think of our entire company as representatives of the brand, from our unique job titles to our office entrance. If you see a Method ad, chances are it features a real Method employee. That baby on the Web site—yup, the child of a proud Method mom. Even the office is designed to serve as a press-friendly backdrop for photo shoots, from the "grass" Ping-Pong room to the green-chef kitchen. Everyone—not just some overpaid models or one chosen spokesperson—is encouraged to be a face of the brand.

Consider our point of view. The more out-of-touch our employees are with the consumer, the more we have to compensate by pouring time and money into efforts like consumer research, quantitative studies, diary panels, and home visits to watch people use the product (we're not kidding). But because our employees are actually creating products for themselves and their families, visionary and revolutionary ideas come straight from the heart. We don't need to ask our consumers what they want because we *are* the consumers. This is why entrepreneurs are so often described as visionary—they start from a place of personal dissatisfaction about something, and they're passionate about improving upon it. Ford loved cars. Fields loved cookies. Pete loved beer. And Peet loved coffee.

Now, granted, we weren't all about soap back in the day, but we did have a passion for design and sustainability. This kind of passion is what fuels the desire to keep improving ahead of our competition and the consumer. Not only do all of our team members help inspire new product ideas, but they help test them too, bringing them home and reporting back on what they think.

For us, this passion starts with striving to keep the majority of advocate touch points in-house by insourcing customer service, advocacy communications, PR, design and creative, etc. We even realigned our hierarchy to ensure we had the right people in charge of guiding the brand, responding to our customers, and integrating any useful feedback. Besides the obvious cost savings, keeping our consumer touch points in-house translates to a nimbler, smarter, more authentic brand.

We're nimbler because we handle new media ourselves. Two-way media is fast and complex, subtle and nuanced. Consider all those corporations that outsource their Twitter accounts to PR firms. Not only is this kind of outsourcing expensive (pay-per-tweet?) and clumsy (can an outsider really speak for you?), it removes the opportunity to engage with the people who matter most to your brand—your consumers. Consumers are also starting to skip searching for customer service contacts when they have a problem, instead going straight to Facebook and Twitter to complain. And if a consumer posts a problem on Facebook, you don't want it sitting there for the world to see for very long.

As we mentioned earlier, we live in a marketing environment that rewards creativity and big ideas instead of big advertising budgets. To take advantage of this shift, we have also structured our marketing department in a fundamentally different way. In the 1940s, major consumer product companies shifted to a brand management system to address the rapidly growing mass market that emerged after World War II. Network television was spreading throughout the nation, the industrial revolution was driving down costs, and companies developed brand management teams trained in the skills of mass media. The theory was that mass advertising would act like a big lever pulling on the P&L, so every business owner should control the marketing.

This model worked beautifully for decades. But as the media world grew more fragmented, it became increasingly difficult to manage the complexity of multichannel communications. Then there's the matter of outside media agencies. No longer do companies work with a single agency; they must rely on a broad group of specialists to juggle print, interactive, PR, and all the other emerging channels. The lack of continuity—not to mention the high turnover in the advertising industry—compounds the problem. Instead of pulling one lever to build a brand, brand managers now are pulling thousands!

TRADITIONAL MARKETING
top-down approach

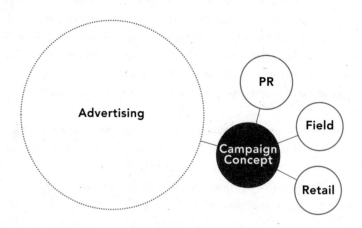

▲ **THE SHIFT FROM COMMAND AND CONTROL TO A CONVERSATION.** ▶
Marketing is no longer about top-down but now bottom-up.

At Method, we addressed these changes by transforming "brand managers" into true business owners. In the process, we put marketing communications in its own department, called Brand Experience. Our pod directors cooperate and interact with Brand Experience in the same way they do with Product Development and with Sales, folding everything into one cohesive business plan. This frees Brand Experience to focus on inspiring advocates. Looking ahead, we plan to continue integrating traditionally outsourced marketing skills. For the time being, here's how we've built Brand Experience:

PR Our second hire at Method was our in-house PR expert. We considered PR a top priority because the role functions in both directions, speaking to consumers about our brand and returning to us with their feedback. Integrating PR in-house not only helps you stay on trend by creating a two-way dialogue with the press, but it also creates authenticity while deepening relationships. The media is always happier to meet with the company directly than with a hired gun. We view members of the press the same way we view retailers: they are collaborators and partners.

TODAY'S MARKETING
bottom-up approach

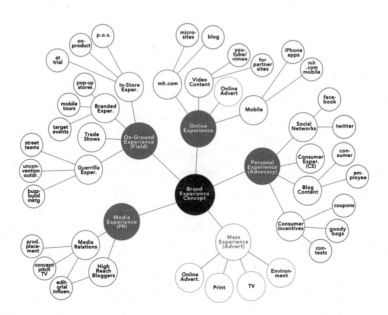

SOCIAL MEDIA If you're working with an outside agency, you're too many phone calls from your consumer. Today marketing happens in real time as a conversation with the consumer. Whether you're running a pop-up retail program or an interactive Web site, bringing your social media department in-house translates into better time management and more savings.

CUSTOMER SERVICE We'll never understand why companies outsource their call centers to India. The customer who is calling has used your product. This isn't just a marketing opportunity; it's a chance to capture new insights, create a raving fan, and even safeguard yourself from legal problems! So while most companies treat customer service as a problem, we've stationed our customer-service specialists right in the heart of our headquarters, alongside our other core departments. We also frequently have everyone in the company take a shift at customer service to keep us all focused on our advocates. So next time you call, don't be surprised if one of us answers.

CREATIVE Modern marketing is about the power of the content, not the power of the spend. Because we view the brand as a collection of experiences that work best when they're all aligned, we placed creatives in business operations roles, where they report directly to the CEO. By putting creatives in responsible leadership positions, where they're in touch with all the expressions of the brand, we've empowered them to build communications stories in real time without heavy-handed oversight by a bureaucratic business layer.

Last but certainly not least, at the heart of branding from the inside out is getting naked. (No, unfortunately, not *that* kind of naked.) In a media-transparent world, providing access to and information about your brand is increasingly a form of marketing in and of itself. Whether we're fielding discontinued-product inquiries from teenage advocates or responding to an ingredient request from a septuagenarian vegan, we have dedicated ourselves to providing access to all the behind-the-scenes details of our brand. We encourage advocates (and skeptics, for that matter) to dig deep into everything from our brand philosophy to our day-to-day operations in order to satisfy their level of interest. Naturally, it's impossible to put all this information on the back of a bottle of soap, so we created Behind the Bottle, a Web site that explores sustainability at Method for those advocates interested in digging deep. It's just one of the ways consumers can peel back the Method onion. Check it out for yourself at www.methodhome.com.

AIM SMALL AND OVERSERVE

If you've been to as many business conferences as we have, you're probably familiar with the "customer pyramid." This is the triangle marketers use to illustrate the different types of consumers—the broad bottom represents less-engaged buyers, and the pinnacle represents the smallest, most loyal group. The objective of our obsession with inspiring advocates is to invert the traditional customer pyramid by growing the group of fanatically devoted consumers at the top, the true Method advocates, into the broadest set, while shrinking the group of semiengaged customers at the bottom. The result: fewer customers (less market share) buying more of your stuff (more wallet share). The idea of flipping the pyramid scares a lot of business leaders because it means focusing on a smaller audience. But in a world with less effective forms of mass media, you have no choice but to focus on a narrower audience to build an efficient marketing model. Today, the riches are in the niches.

There are several reasons why this inverted model works. First, we all know it's cheaper to get an existing customer to try more of your products than to acquire a new one, and in our case, we play in a $24 billion sandbox (in the United States alone). If we can achieve just 5 percent market share, we will have built a billion-dollar brand! Overserving a niche will actually create a much larger long-term market than any vague overture to the broad middle. It's the lighthouse effect. Aiming small creates an aspirational halo—a beacon of shared values and brand traits that draws others in. Apple with creative professionals; Nike with track runners; Red Bull with ravers—we challenge you to find a large successful brand today that didn't start by overserving a niche audience. The same is true with the music industry, in which artists must build a small but loyal following until

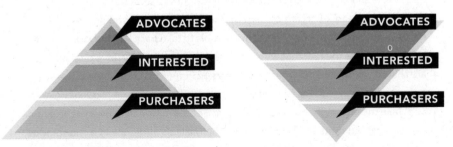

▲ **FLIP THE PYRAMID.** Today's media environment requires overserving a small audience. Think wallet share, not market share.

word spreads. Ever been to a LCD Soundsystem show or seen Flight of the Conchords in concert? Our point exactly. Big companies have a lousy batting average when it comes to launching new brands—mostly because they lack the patience to build a loyal following with a core audience.

Finally, aiming small generates extreme loyalty. There will always be someone with a lower price, especially if you're offering a premium product. But a loyal audience sticks with you when other brands are offering a temporary deal. Advocates boost your adoption rates because they are willing to take a risk on your new ideas—essential to a business like ours, in which success is dependent on being the category thought leader.

We aim small by focusing on our three archetypes—true greenies, trendsetters, and status seekers. Together they represent about 27 percent of U.S. households, giving us a focused audience we can serve better than anyone else while also allowing us a big enough sandbox to build toward a billion-dollar brand. The common interests driving these archetypes are passion for the environment, health in the home, and great design. It's rare to have a brand that attracts consumers for a wide variety of reasons, but that diversity speaks to the breadth and depth of our brand appeal.

CREATE A MOVEMENT

Representatives of other brands often ask, "How do I harness my following through Facebook or all these other social media tools?" Many companies fall back on the old top-down, command-and-control tendencies, thinking of their audience as an army that needs to be deployed. Good luck with that. To connect, you need to treat customers the same way you would your friends. After all, they're following your brand because they share its values. Your goal should be to reinforce those shared values through your behaviors and interactions and thus inspire advocacy. Instead of trying to deploy them, focus on providing content that enhances those values and give them the tools to take part. At Method, our advocates appreciate the fact that we care for the environment and love design. These are shared values, and we create marketing programs that deliver on these values in a beneficial way (such as sending them copies of our first book, *Squeaky Green*).

Take the late-night battle between Jay Leno and Conan O'Brien as an example. Leno is old media—speaking to his half-asleep audience in a monologue, while Conan has learned that performing means engaging. When he does standup, Conan encourages the audience to tweet questions, and fans rallied around him when he was ousted from NBC ("I'm with Coco!"). Conan has over 2 million Twitter followers and over a million friends on Facebook, proof that Team Coco fans see themselves as participants, not viewers.

When your goal is to inspire advocates, marketing communications are about creating a movement. In a traditional advertising campaign, you talk about yourself, but a movement requires you to talk about your advocates. Movements always start with a small group of deeply passionate people, and this must be true inside and outside the company. Movements have shared ownership and powerful identities. Campaigns have a beginning and an end, while movements can live forever.

To create a movement, we focus communications around two key ingredients: *change* and *participation.* Every marketing initiative should draw attention to some kind of change—a change in our products, our industry, or the world at large—and should inspire participation from our advocates—inviting them to engage with the brand and share control in how campaigns take shape and spread in the market.

Motivating change is not too different from running a political campaign. Ever wonder why our airwaves are dominated by negative political ads come election season? Because they work! Politicians know it's far easier to rally people against something that's already out there than to introduce them to something new. As a brand striving to create social change, we face a challenge similar to that of a politician trying to get elected. We frequently think of our marketing as a political campaign with the goal trying to get a core group of advocates to rally for change.

But the secret to winning an election or creating change is that you can't just be against something. You also have to be for something. You have to explain why your alternative vision is better. We try to focus our messaging on both of these levers simultaneously by showing what we are for as well as what we are against. For example, we are against dirty but for clean. Whenever we point out what we want to eliminate (toxins, laundry jugs, the smell of bleach), we always propose an easy replacement with what we want more of (natural ingredients, concentrated bottles, and pink grapefruit scent). You have to give your advocates hope and make change easy.

At Method, we have to educate our consumers about questionable toxins in the trusted brand their moms used, but we don't want to scare them or turn them off, so we present our products as a good, safe, *clean* alternative. One tool we've found effective is our Dirty Little Secrets campaign, in which we expose some of the nasty things that make up some of the most trusted cleaning brands.

for a
jug-free
america.

every day, jugs are sold right under our very noses.
heavy jugs that are hurting arms and spilling blue liquid
in laundry rooms throughout this great nation of ours.
it's time to stop this. let's stand together and get rid
of jugs once and for all.

how do we do this? method® laundry detergent. it finds
stains in a whole new way to get your clothes amazingly
clean. the secret is our patent pending formula that's
so frickin' concentrated, 50 loads fits in a teeny bottle.
and if that's not enough, we ditched that messy cap
for an easy-dose pump so the revolution can begin
in your laundry room.

are you with us, america? let's get off the jugs and
get clean. learn more at **methodlaundry.com**

method
LAUNDRY DETERGENT

m method
people against dirty

are you
a jug
addict?

m method
people against dirty

say no
to jugs.

m method
people against dirty

▲ **LAUNDRY REVOLUTION.** Inspiring advocates is about creating a movement
built on purpose. It's not what they buy, but what they buy into.

Take fabric softener. Do you know the chief ingredient that makes your clothes
feel so soft? It's tallow—beef fat. That's right, the goodness of beef fat in your
Egyptian cotton. Dirty. We gave the world a vegan fabric softener, which inspired
our advocates, especially those concerned about animal cruelty. In fact, PETA
liked that idea (and others) so much, they honored the two of us with their Person
of the Year awards in 2006. This association, while an honor in and of itself, is also
a great marketing tool because it gives us a stamp of approval from the world's
most trusted animal-rights group.

We draw inspiration from our advocates and new ideas from our idols. One
of these is Adam Morgan, author of *Eating the Big Fish*. Among Morgan's more
powerful ideas for challenger brands is "identifying your monster"—a common
enemy you and the customer can bond over. As it takes time to introduce your

message, creating a monster is a great way to speed things up by starting a conversation with your advocates.

For example, when we launched our innovative laundry detergent, it was so foreign to the category that we needed to show people the change it could represent in their lives. We needed a foil. In this case, the perfect foil was the ubiquitous laundry jug. So we created a "Say No to Jugs" advertising campaign that painted these ugly behemoths as monsters while our simple, no-mess pump became a hero.

Then there was the daisy story—the monster opportunity came to us. For years, we've used a daisy in our packaging and marketing as a way to illustrate that our products are gentle and natural. Then we opened the mail one day to find a big fat cease-and-desist letter from our friends across the bay at Clorox. Apparently, Clorox's Green Works line also used a daisy in its marketing, and the brand was threatening legal action. You read that right: Clorox was claiming it owned the daisy, a universal icon of peace and beauty. (Never mind the fact that we had been using it for over five years.) Up until then, it had never even occurred to us to register the daisy; to be honest, we kind of assumed Mother Nature held that trademark.

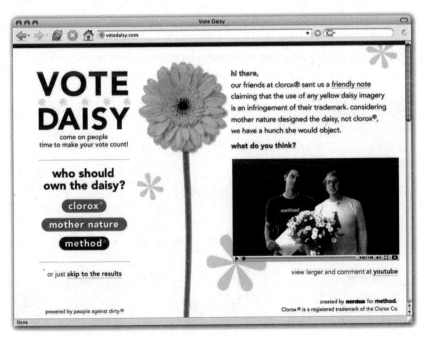

▲ **INVITE PARTICIPATION.** With a small legal budget, we invited our advocates to decide who should own the daisy in the court of public opinion.

Naturally, we weren't about to give up our rights to use the daisy, but we didn't want to spend a lot on legal bills either. Inspired by Ben & Jerry's "one-man picket line" in front of rival Pillsbury headquarters ("What's the doughboy afraid of?"), we turned to our advocates. Our Internet appeal: Help us battle large corporations that claim to own nature (can you spot the monster?). Then we sent a charming letter to Clorox: Isn't it silly for us to fight over a flower? Why don't we let the people decide who should own the daisy? Enter votedaisy.com, a microsite where we posted Clorox's cease-and-desist letter alongside a video of us explaining the situation and an invitation to vote on who should own the daisy—Method, Clorox, or Mother Earth.

Within hours of launch, votedaisy.com was picked up by the *New York Times*. Thousands of people voted, and naturally, Mother Earth won by a landslide. And in a testament to advocate loyalty, hundreds of lawyers sent us free legal advice, assuring us that we were in the right. Suffice it to say, we never heard back from Clorox.

ERROR AUTOPSY: SHINY SUDS

For all we've talked about the scary toxins that go into most cleaning products, you'd never be able to tell if you just looked at their labels. Under U.S. law, companies are required to disclose ingredients for products that you digest or apply to your skin (food, beverages, and personal care products). But mum's the word

▲ **SHARE CONTROL.** To support the Household Product Labeling Act , we asked people to rethink how "dirty" their cleaning products may be.

when it comes to home-care products. On top of that, only one in every thousand chemicals in the consumer market has been tested for long-term human health effects. Yeah, this is a big problem.

At Method, we will tell you every molecule in every one of our products. That's because, unlike our competitors, we have nothing to hide. But then, in 2009 senators Al Franken and Steve Israel introduced the Household Product Labeling Act, which would require companies like ours to tell consumers what's in their products.

Spotting the perfect opportunity to mobilize our advocates and bring attention to an important issue, we sprang into action. Partnering with Droga5, we created a viral video spoofing traditional cleaning ads with a fake brand called Shiny Suds (enter the villain).

Our video opened like a traditional cleaning ad (obnoxious jingle and all). A woman watched in delight as animated bubbles went to work giving her tub that fantastic shiny look. Fade to black and the scene cuts to the next morning, when the women returns for her morning shower and is shocked to find the bubbles are still there! These "dirty" bubbles explain that they are toxic residue, left over from that "thorough" cleaning, and they go on to annoy the woman with catcalls as she tries to shower. The video ends by asking consumers if they know what is in their cleaners and showing the URL of a microsite where they can instantly shoot e-mails to their senators asking them to support the bill.

We knew the video contained content that some might consider mildly sexual, but we wanted to convey a sense of invasion so people would understand how important the issue was. We were careful to cast a confident woman, we showed less skin than a Victoria's Secret ad, and we made sure the bubbles came across as more annoying than menacing. We even shared it with both Al Franken's and Steve Israel's offices to make sure they were comfortable with the content, and we previewed it to a live audience of over a thousand people at a conference forty-eight hours before sending the video out. Live audience approval and positive press in the New York Times the following day made us confident that we were on the right track.

On a Wednesday morning, we e-mailed the video to our advocates and hoped our message would spread. And spread it did! Within an hour, we had thousands of views, and a few days later, over a million! In one week, it became the thirty-fourth most-often-viewed video on YouTube. It had almost a five-star rating and was picked up by hundreds of online news sites with positive reviews.

Sounds like a huge hit, so why is this an error autopsy? Well, we learned the lesson that when you cede control of the conversation, you may not like where the conversation goes. As the video neared 2 million views, we started receiving angry messages on our customer service line and blog. It turned out that some individuals' groups felt we were condoning bad behavior with our dirty little cartoon bubbles.

Our intent in this campaign was to raise awareness for transparency in cleaning product labeling, not make people feel creeped out by watching naughty bubbles. However, we understood the concerns associated with the video and removed it from YouTube and all other controlled sources. The decision came down to our values, and even though we knew our brand would never intentionally do any harm, we listened to what individuals were saying. In the end, we learned that when you create a conversation, you might not always like where it goes, but as long as you stick to your values, your advocates will stick by your side.

OUR INSPIRE-ADVOCATES MUSE: THE LADS AT INNOCENT DRINKS

Hop a plane across the pond, walk into any store selling beverages, and there on the shelf you'll find a charming little smoothie brand called Innocent—the closest thing we have to a sister company. The founders, Richard Reed, Adam Balon, and Jon Wright, share our backgrounds in advertising and science, we're the same age, and we founded our companies within a year of each other. The Monday morning huddle, the Astroturf-carpeted Ping-Pong room, the People and Environment Department—these are just a few of the many ideas we've stolen from Innocent over the years.

Innocent is also the master in treating everything as media and leveraging every touch point. From their view, the label on the bottle is serious media, representing 2 million potential views, based on the number of bottles they ship per week. Flip the bottle over and you just might be surprised to find little sentences like *Help, I'm trapped in a plastic bottle factory!* (Hmm, we might have to steal that idea too.)

Similar to Method, Innocent is driven by a purpose larger than making money. Innocent is on a mission to help people live and eat more healthily, offering drinks and food that make it easy and enjoyable to get the recommended daily allowance of fruits and vegetables. It's rare that Innocent runs any form of marketing that does not invite participation, from its former Fruitstock festivals to the more recent tactic of asking people to create its next ad. Ask anyone in the United Kingdom about Innocent, and you're likely to hear them use the word *love* while describing the brand. So much of this love comes from Innocent's ability to inspire advocates with a trustful, charming voice. Innocent speaks directly and honestly in such a lovable tone that you can't help but become an instant fan of their cause.

Their brand voice inspires us, so much so, in fact, that we stole the man responsible for that voice, Dan Germain, and brought him over as an exchange student. The idea was simple: Give us Dan for a week, and we'll send you one of our best and brightest in return.

Dan spent the week helping us improve our voice. During that week, he passed on the best marketing advice he'd ever heard: Write for one person. Talk about aiming small! The secret to a great brand voice isn't just using your own voice—it's using that voice to speak authentically, the same way you speak to your family and friends. So how are we doing? Has Dan taught us well?

▲ **THE VOICE OF INNOCENCE.** Dan Germain, the man who taught us to always write for one person to keep copy personal.

obsession

3

BE A GREEN GIANT

personalize sustainability to inspire change on a grand scale

WE FOUNDED METHOD ON THE IDEA THAT business, as the largest and most powerful institution on the planet, has the greatest opportunity to create solutions to our environmental and health crises. Since the dawn of the industrial age, business has traded people's health and the state of the planet for growth and profit, but it doesn't need to be so. After having spent a number of years working on environmental issues at the Carnegie Institution, Adam grew increasingly frustrated with preaching to the converted. He was working on cutting-edge science that showed that humanity needed to change its relationship with nature, only to have that science published in obscure journals read by already concerned scientists. He was convinced that business could be a better tool for change than policy because it reached more people, every day. and (ironically) it was more democratic. But the vision was not business as we know it today. It was a vision for a fundamentally and profoundly different kind of business: business redesigned. And so we created a different type of company, one that makes a different kind of product in a different way.

Today the green movement is teetering between revolution and irrelevance. The explosion in green products, services, and marketing over the past ten years has generated a lot of confusion and mistrust, which risk undermining the environmental movement at large. The rise of "greenwashing"—unscrupulous companies making exaggerated claims about their products' environmental benefits—has driven a lot of consumer confusion about what is truly green and created a green bubble, as retailers and the media capitalize on consumer trends. This confusion is feeding the biggest threat to the green movement yet: consumer apathy.

With each new earnest headline about the green movement, consumers grow more and more inured. Scolded for buying bottled water, you buy the Nalgene water bottle, only to discover that the Nalgene bottles contain phthalates (a class of chemicals called endocrine disrupters, which accumulate in the body and mimic hormones. So you switch to the SIGG bottle, only to discover that it's lined with bisphenol-A, which—you guessed it—wreaks havoc on your hormones as well. Rather than allow consumers to make informed choices, this information overload is making them feel more helpless than ever.

Amid all the noise, most of us just want a trusted name to tell us what's what. Perhaps it should come as no surprise, then, that Americans readily accept "green" products from some of the world's largest polluters. After all, these same polluters regularly show up in media rankings as the greenest companies in America. If you look at *Newsweek*'s Green Rankings, you find an alarming cor-

▲ **GREEN PRODUCTS COME ONLY FROM GREEN COMPANIES.** At Method, we work to bring green to the mainstream instead of preaching to the converted.

relation between a company's score and the amount of money spent on green marketing.

That's why we believe it's important to be a "dark green" business (with deeply held environmental principles) inside a "light green" shell (with an approachable and friendly appeal). At Method, sustainability is simply part of everything we do, not a marketing position. By adhering to a philosophy of deep sustainability behind the scenes, we can focus on delivering the best darn cleaners out there, green or otherwise, and let our product experience and our brand personality delight customers rather than beat them over the head with a message about sustainability. Rather than wear our commitment to sustainability on our sleeves, we try to make it just another aspect of the quality of every Method product. So far, it's been an enduring recipe for success, one that keeps our brand identity positive and optimistic and drives us to build and innovate even as the pretender green brands slowly go the way of the dodo. Most important, this approach lets us bring green to the mainstream by making more sustainable things that people *want* to buy, instead of trying to pull the mainstream toward green by getting people to buy green products that require sacrifice.

Why the optimism in the face of all the greenwashing? The transparency of the Internet and the openness of social media tools are already exposing the differences between corporations' private and public faces, driving the focus away from what you say to what you do. We've practiced what we've preached since the beginning, so we're confident that, when it comes to being truly authentic, we have an edge over our competitors.

Sustainability is an opportunity. On an increasingly small, hot, and crowded planet, smart companies are identifying new ways to gain a competitive edge. Beyond the obvious impact to your environment, sustainability will affect your business and your career. If you're looking to launch a business, green is either going to be an asset or a liability. Unlike business trends that deal with ephemeral consumer behaviors, sustainability is about how we use resources to improve the quality of our lives and enhance the existence of our species. This new reality is one where the interests of science and business intersect, and it ain't going away. Ignoring it will cost you.

THE PARADOX OF SUSTAINABLE INNOVATION

It isn't hard to imagine a fully sustainable product—one with no negative impact on the environment or the social condition. So why doesn't one exist? The answer lies in the most crucial aspect of innovation that people usually forget: people.

In order for an innovation to be truly innovative, people have to use it. A lot of people. As green innovators, nothing is more frustrating to us than hearing about an innovative new product only a few privileged people can get their hands on. That's not innovation. That's obscurity. Which is to say, technology and creativity aren't the most important components of innovation—*adoption* is.

Consider refill stations, an innovative development in the cleaning products industry in the United Kingdom. Refill stations enable you to bring an empty spray bottle to a store, scan the bar code, and refill your bottle like a cup of soda. You get a refill without having to buy a whole new bottle and trigger, and the retailer isn't stuck shipping a bunch of plastic around the country. Seems like a no-brainer, right?

Maybe on paper, but the idea wasn't conceived with adoption in mind. How many times have you forgotten your reusable shopping bags when you make a trip to the store? Say you just got to the store and remembered you're out of cleaner. What are you going to do? Buy a new bottle. Bottom line, in a category like cleaning, which consumers want to think about as little as possible, asking them to make an extra effort is the kiss of death.

The best innovations are self-educating. Their designs make it obvious that the behavior change required will make life better. In contrast to refill stations, we've had tremendous success with our line of refill pouches because the benefit of the product and the way to use it are simultaneously clear to consumers.

The important thing about this refill pouch product is not so much its sustainability benefits. While it creates an admirable 80 percent reduction in plastic use, one could point out that a refill station does this and also saves on the transport of water. The important thing is that we have gotten a large group of people off the habit of buying a new bottle and trigger every time they run out of cleaner. That change of habit allows us to innovate again. Maybe it will allow us to develop a concentrate or refill-at-shelf format that is incrementally more sustainable and adoptable. When we do, however, we will focus our efforts on solving the convenience issues so that the format is not asking for more effort from the consumer, but rather making the product easier and more delightful to use.

The fascinating part about this phenomenon of serial innovation is that it includes and is dependent on people. It is exactly these small, intermediary steps that become the steady march toward a more sustainable future. The pundits and dilettantes will stand on the sidelines and critique the market, saying that we need more demonstrably sustainable products and we need people to realize they *must* use them. But they miss the point. Until someone wants to use something, really *wants* to, change cannot be created.

This brings us to our next topic—getting people to *want* to use your product without forcing them to sacrifice or change their habits.

GREED IS GOOD

Greed captures the essence of the evolutionary spirit.

—Gordon Gekko, in *Wall Street* (1987).

Let us be the first to say it: Gordon Gekko would have been a greenie. Why would the icon of greed be green? For the same reason so many companies all over the world are going green these days: The push toward sustainability is demonstrating a direct positive impact on the bottom line.

The unquestioned belief that green is going to cost you more money is less valid every day. Much as Gekko said of greed, the green movement in today's business ecosystem is driving a number of positive behaviors. Beyond environmental improvements, the financial argument for sustainability gets stronger every day—from innovative packaging solutions that save materials and money to efficiencies in shipping.

Moreover, green companies are learning to incorporate nascent green practices in order to create and leverage new and distinct competitive advantages. Major retailers are now recycling millions of tons of cardboard, capturing revenue where they once sustained costs in shipping waste to the landfill. Many of the world's largest distributors now move greater proportions of material via rail instead of trucks, saving fuel and labor. Best of all, they're doing it all in a way that would have made Gekko grin: by making it selfish.

Allow us to explain. In business, as in life, selfish motivations often align with philanthropic ends, inspiring dramatic independent action and social change. Of course, selfishness is the last thing most of us generally think about when we think about the green movement. Selflessness and sacrifice are more likely to come to mind. But people are tired of hearing the same environmental guilt trips. *Turn off your lights, unplug your appliances, don't drink bottled water.* Enough, already. Since when is Mother Earth such a boring old nag? She doesn't have to be, of course. Sustainability can be sexy. It can be savvy. And it works best when it's selfish. Hence "Making It Selfish" is our favorite sustainability irony—we're employing selfishness as the primary means of achieving selfless results.

When most of us think about the environmental revolution, we tend to picture long-haired crazies following leaders in hair shirts. Granted, these folks are out there. We'd be lying if we said we didn't know a few people who repurpose their bathwater, sew their own clothes, and keep their all-natural deodorant in the fridge. If it's yellow, let it mellow? Yeah, we're cool with that. But frankly, the self-righteous green leaders we know are more about status than principle—they're elitists, not egalitarians. And as the green movement has become more mainstream, many of those leaders have retreated further to the fringes instead of celebrating and encouraging the success of the movement. And no revolution can sustain itself by staying on the fringe.

We want to create a revolution driven by the armchair revolutionaries who make up the silent majority. This is the fundamental design challenge at the heart of Method, how to align selfish interests (the financial, the visceral) with selfless ones (the social and environmental). The success of the green movement won't come from attempting to convert everyone into a crazy rebel. That's why we've never understood the do-it-for-the-environment ethic—it's inherently limiting. Leading a revolution of casual environmentalists requires aligning people's deep, personal interests with their broad social and environmental concerns, making the selfish, most appealing choice the green choice.

As far as we're concerned, it doesn't matter if a consumer chooses our pouch refills because they have 80 percent less plastic or buys our hand wash because they like the pretty purple bottle. People have asked us, "Doesn't it bother you that some people buy Method and don't know it's green?" Sure, we would prefer that people know our bigger mission, but the earth can't tell the difference! By inspiring people who wouldn't otherwise choose green, we may eventually lead them to read the back of the bottle (or go to our Web site) and learn why the aesthetically appealing choice also happens to be the responsible one. And even if they don't, their purchase of a green product is still driving real change.

Making green selfish isn't just about consumers, either. No matter what your industry, green needs to be relevant and motivating to everyone else who touches your business, from your colleagues to your competitors. The key to motivating people to be green is not to try to convince them that it's the right thing to do. It's much easier and more effective to find a way to align it with their existing motivations—It'll save you money! It's good for you! It's fun to use!

Don't get us wrong. We're not green because it's on trend but because we believe it's important. Selfishness aside, the green movement is about the long-term survival of our species. Like it or not, it's the truth—which is why Being a Green Giant is our most important obsession when it comes to the world at large. It's why we started Method in the first place—to create positive change through business by inspiring a happy, healthy home revolution. Touchy-feely? Sure. Important enough to merit a place in every company's guiding principles? Without question.

That said, like many environmentally friendly companies, we've wrestled with how much we want to be labeled a green company. Being typecast as a green company alone sells short the innovative technology, leading performance, and aesthetic beauty inherent in each of our products. In fact, in the beginning, we actually hid some of our green attributes from investors and consumers because they would have assumed our products weren't as effective as others on the market. In order to overcome misperceptions, we have to appeal to the selfish desires of everyone who comes in contact with our business. Below is a guide to how we do it.

MAKING IT SELFISH . . . FOR OUR CONSUMERS

In the past, the self-interested choice has generally been the nongreen choice. Gas-guzzling SUVs. High-fat, high-carb foods. Disposable everything. If you look at humanity throughout the ages, you can see that in places where people had to choose between acting morally or acting selfishly, they generally chose the latter.

When it comes to choosing green, what's the average person most likely to do—buy something that benefits them as an individual or something that contributes to society? Come on, we all know the answer. A personal need or desire will almost always trump a collective, existential one. (Think horsepower versus emissions or leisure time versus charity work.) Don't get us wrong, there are millions of do-gooders who make the right choices on a daily basis, but there just aren't enough of them out there to save this little planet we're spinning on.

Case in point: Back in the 1980s, the argument for the organic movement went something like, "Eat organic food because pesticides are bad for the environment." Most people yawned. Years later, the argument shifted—"Eat organic food because it's bad to put pesticides in your body." This time, people took notice. Hormones and antibiotics in our milk?! Women started worrying about their children. Men started worrying about moobs (er, man boobs). The general public wasn't willing to give up cheaper milk when the environment was the only casualty, but when cheap milk threatened our personal health (or manhood), we listened. Today, it's hard to find a grocery store that doesn't offer organic milk.

The circumstances were no different in cleaning. Use an ecofriendly product because it's good for the earth? Boring. Consumers might have tried it once, but when the product was twice as expensive and half as effective as the ordinary cleaners, they gave up. After all, people don't actually see the environmental damage they're causing, so why should they sacrifice convenience and cleaning power—especially when their neighbor is already dumping bleach down the drain anyway? The impact of our purchasing decisions is abstract and easy to ignore until you shift the argument to something personal—like toxic chemicals in our homes or bodies. Then, suddenly, it becomes much more relevant and real.

With this in mind, we have changed the cleaning conversation, shifting the focus to the health of our families, our pets, and ourselves. One of our recent advertising campaigns for household cleaners talked about improving the air

---

A few years ago, we were in London doing press interviews for the launch of our toilet-bowl cleaner (yeah, it's a glamorous life). Now, the UK press has a reputation for being highly skeptical, and when Eric touted the product's nontoxic properties, one journalist challenged him. "If it's so nontoxic," she asked, "would you drink it?" Not one to back down from a challenge, Eric poured a shot and slammed it. Soon after, the head of PR in the UK and one of the journalists in the crowd joined in. Needless to say, it would be bad PR if a couple of Method employees got sick from drinking a product (not recommended), especially if a writer for a major UK newspaper did as well. Promptly upon exiting the interview, the following text exchange occurred.

Eric: Hey Adam, in London and just drank the toilet bowl cleaner. Along with Louise. And a high profile journalist. We'll be fine, right?

Adam: well, it would not have been my first choice.

Eric: thank you captain obvious. Seriously, We'll be fine right???

Adam: Yes. But next time try the bathroom cleaner. It's less minty.

▲ **WHERE DO YOU END AND WHERE DOES YOUR HOME BEGIN?**
Deep down, you're nontoxic and biodegradable, and your home wants to stay
that way, too.

quality inside your home instead of outside it. Our call to action to the armchair
revolutionaries has been "Save yourself. Save the world." In that order. To strike
a balance between being a dark green company with a light green shell, we
ensure that the selfish choice for the consumer *is* the responsible choice, and we
build that kind of consumer trust through a deep commitment to sustainability
and providing transparency in everything we do. Besides being honest in our
marketing, we've always "kept it personal," promoting the message that Method
is good for your *home* environment (little *e*) first, and the Environment (big *E*)
after that.

Altruistic brands trying to create change in the world must be able to make
the issues relatable at a personal and intimate level. This means answering the
question "What's in it for me?" People are inspired by causes that are connected
to them—like the people, pets, or places they already care deeply about. If a
cause feels too far removed from people's lives, it is difficult to inspire them to
take action. The best way to motivate them is by tying an issue to something that
they already care about at a personal level. Big issues need to be broken into
human-size chunks. So while melting glaciers and drowning polar bears are too
distant to inspire all but the most devoted climate defenders, the impending

▲ MAKE THE CAUSE RELEVANT AND RELATABLE. At Method, we try to shift the conversation from use method to save the environment to use method to save your home environment.

disappearance of a favorite local beach will motivate and mobilize an entire community to action.

This more personal, intimate approach wouldn't be possible without radical transparency. Traditional corporations may shudder at the prospect of opening themselves to the world, but radical transparency is a critical means of building trust between you and your customers—or in our case, advocates. It starts with your most loyal, engaged customers—those curious enough to do their research and hold you accountable to your ideals and objectives. As your reputation and credibility gather momentum, transparency reinforces your connection with casual customers and attracts new advocates. When you're dealing with advocates like ours, who understand that true sustainability is more a goal than a reality, transparency is the best way of showing progress—and any company that is truly committed to sustainability must be committed to continually improving. So we are completely transparent about our shortcomings—discussing our failures and impacts openly with our consumers. (Have something to share? E-mail us at info@methodhome.com, or, better yet, call us sometime at 1-866-9METHOD.) We are the first to tell you what we are not doing well and where we want to improve.

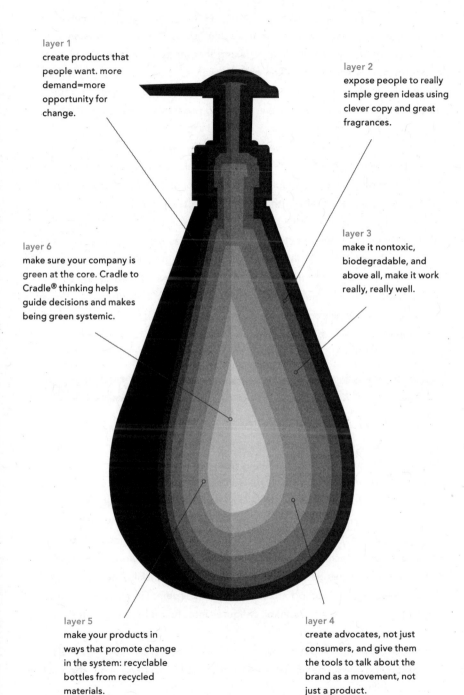

layer 1
create products that people want. more demand=more opportunity for change.

layer 2
expose people to really simple green ideas using clever copy and great fragrances.

layer 3
make it nontoxic, biodegradable, and above all, make it work really, really well.

layer 6
make sure your company is green at the core. Cradle to Cradle® thinking helps guide decisions and makes being green systemic.

layer 5
make your products in ways that promote change in the system: recyclable bottles from recycled materials.

layer 4
create advocates, not just consumers, and give them the tools to talk about the brand as a movement, not just a product.

The beautiful thing about transparency is that it creates engagement. Consumers see what we do well and what we don't do so well, and they push us to get better. In turn, we push them—coaxing them to test and adopt new ideas and formulas instead of the token green-tweak here or there. It's a symbiotic relationship between us and our advocates, driving rapid change and radical innovation. It's why the label on every Method product says DESIGNED BY AND FOR PEOPLE AGAINST DIRTY.

That close connection between the company and consumer is key for any green company. After all, what's the point of making a truly innovative green product if people are too intimidated, confused, or uninterested to use it? Back in 2000, the general belief was that green products were supposed to be ugly, smelly, and ineffective. In order to engage the consumer, we flipped the model. We asked ourselves, why can't green products be as beautiful as nature? And do you really need to smell like the earth to love it? Of course not! Adopting a spoonful-of-sugar philosophy, we introduced high design with deep sustainability, helping change the paradigm of green products. Call it eco-chic. We're not exactly sure we were the first to define the term, but if you know of anyone who coined it before us, let us know!

MAKING IT SELFISH . . . FOR OUR TEAM MEMBERS

At Method, we refer to the process of integrating sustainability into everyone's role as *greenskeeping*. It sounds like just another buzzword, but it's radically different from the way most companies treat sustainability. Most make sustainability a department. It sounds like a good idea, but if you turn sustainability into a marginal function—one that only a small group of people is responsible for—you'll get marginal results. We believe that the only way to achieve breakthrough results is to get every head in the game. At Method, sustainability is everyone's job. To achieve this, we teach it, train it, and develop it in every Person Against Dirty, just as you would any basic business skill. The people who drive this process at Method are called greenskeepers. Greenskeepers teach our team members how sustainability figures into their jobs and give them the tools to pursue it.

Among the first things we teach new hires at Method are the core beliefs of greenskeeping, the fundamental tenets that form the backbone of our approach to sustainability and the nucleus of our "dark green" core.

The first is our belief in the precautionary principle. Ever see the label warning SAFE IF USED AS DIRECTED? This is the traditional approach, focused on risk—it's "safe" to use hazardous chemicals as long as you're not exposed to too many of them. In contrast, the precautionary principle doesn't accept that level of risk. It looks at the risk of using a certain chemical or material by way of one basic equation:

RISK = HAZARD x EXPOSURE

It doesn't take a mathematician to realize that if you keep the hazard at zero or very low, an individual's exposure can still be very high without raising the risk. In light of all the reports of the negative health effects and environmental damage caused by chemicals deemed "safe if used as directed," we believe focusing on hazard, not risk, is the only real way to design products. This approach requires assessing every single material we use for environmental quality and human safety. Yes, it's laborious. Nevertheless, over time, this approach has generated a library of safe ingredients and materials that we know produce inherently better products, and a long list of ingredients and materials that we will never use, even though most traditional cleaning companies still do.

The second core belief of greenskeeping is our belief in reincarnation—using materials that have a past, present, and future. One of the keys to sustain-

▲ **EVERYONE IS A GREENSKEEPER.** Each person is taught the ins and outs of sustainability and how to integrate it into their job.

ability is understanding the source, use, and disposal of everything we use. Traditionally, the best way to assess all of this is with something called a life-cycle assessment (LCA), a detailed analysis of every cost and impact involved in sourcing, implementing, and recycling (or disposing of) every ingredient and material. Unfortunately, LCAs are far too expensive and time-consuming to apply to every material a company uses—you could write a PhD thesis in the time it takes to do an LCA on one petroleum-based ingredient. So we've simplified the LCA process by bringing in Dr. Michael Braungart, a German design chemist and author of the seminal work about sustainable design, *Cradle to Cradle: Remaking the Way We Make Things*. Cradle to cradle is a design philosophy based on five simple tenets that guide the design and creation of anything: Use biological and technical nutrients, design closed material loops, emit water clean enough to drink, use energy from the sun, and practice social fairness.

Now, here's the most important part of the reincarnation principal: rather than keeping all that information in the lab, we pass on everything we learn from Dr. Braungart to our team members. Marketing, customer support, design, janitorial—everyone. Every team member at Method is trained to recognize that natural ingredients, for example, have a past as things that actually grow in the ground, such as plants, while petroleum-based ingredients come from a barrel of oil. They also know that truly recyclable plastic can become another bottle, while PVC will sit in a landfill and leach phthalates into our groundwater. Whether you're a scientist in a white lab coat or a marketer in all black, we have a common language that allows us to discuss and improve the health and environmental profile of everything we design. Below, a few greenskeeping techniques we teach our employees to ensure that sustainability remains a part of everyone's job:

SHINING THE LIGHT One of the hardest things to do is get people to understand the impact of their decisions, both at work and at home. For example, most people have never gone (and never will go) to a wastewater treatment plant or a recycling center, but our employees have. Is this because we like to show them a good time? No, it's because when you visit places like this, you can literally see the impact you have on the world around you. At the recycling center, it's the types of bottles (some of which you thought were recyclable) that get kicked off the conveyor belt and into the landfill pile. At the water-treatment center, it's the damage done by pouring bleach down the drain. Field trips like this give people an image they can take with them to help them make more informed decisions at their desk. Whether you're a technical, visual, or philosophical person, actually seeing your decisions in action hammers home the consequences. We all collectively own this problem, and the onus is on us to fix it.

DIGGING DEEPER (THE DIFFERENCE BETWEEN RECYCL*ABLE* AND RECYC*LED*) To the average consumer, a distinction like this may not appear to matter much, but our team members work with this kind of issue every day when sourcing materials and examining the life cycles of our products. Take the recycling center example above. Many of the so-called green cleaning brands are packaged in white PET, a plastic that has become de rigueur for green cleaning brands because white represents "cleanliness" and "naturalness." While it's the same recyclable material that water bottles are made of, once you dye it white, you've doomed it to the landfill. That's because municipal recycling centers can't distinguish white PET from other commonly recycled materials, like milk cartons (made of HDPE). The PET is sent to the milk carton recycler, who sees it as an "impurity" in his supply and throws it away. It's a cruel irony: the color most often chosen to communicate "greenness" is precisely what causes it to be less green. Method's designers know this, and we don't use white PET.

▲ ROLE MODELS IN BOTTLES. Method's bottles are made from 100 percent old plastic. There is so much plastic in the world, we just figured we would use that instead of making more.

GIVING THEM THE TOOLS It's not enough to simply teach people about sustainability; you have to give them tools to integrate it into their work. We provide tools for integrating sustainability into every job—analytical tools, like software to help our load planners lower the carbon footprint of our shipments, and qualitative tools, like marketing surveys to help our copywriters understand how green claims are seen by dark greenies and by outsiders. We have decision-making tools to help our packaging engineers choose the right materials and quantitative tools that our manufacturing specialists use to eliminate the use of water in making our product. Regardless of function, everyone is equipped and empowered to help make Method more sustainable.

Ultimately, nothing is more effective than putting employees in the field and doing work in the community. Fieldwork is the most immediate way to connect the work we're doing to the impacts we have on the world around us. As part of our Ecomaniacs program, each employee does several days of work in the community every year, either solo or with fellow Method employees as part of a company effort (we organize a number of annual in-house volunteer programs). This way, Method can choose to support activities that matter to us as a company, and employees can choose efforts that are important to them individually. They might work with Compass, an agency that provides housing for homeless San Franciscans (and uses Method products to make those houses cleaner and healthier) or with Root Division, which uses the imaginative power of art to educate and inspire children. Giving back to the community instills in our team members a deeper sense of purpose when they're selecting green chemicals to make a product healthier or putting the finishing touches on a design that will make our customers' lives that much safer and easier.

BROWN-BAG SERIES To keep team members' minds fresh and invigorated, we frequently bring in practitioners from other parts of the world of sustainability to tell us how they do their jobs. Though we call this the Brown-bag series (because it's always held during a BYO lunch), the speaker schedule reads like a Who's Who of the design and sustainability cognoscenti, including Tim Brown, CEO of IDEO, and renowned green architect Bill McDonough. It's an intimate interaction that fuels thoughtful work and helps make each and every Person Against Dirty a greenskeeper.

▲ **PEOPLE AGAINST DIRTY AT WORK.** We are fortunate to work alongside team members who share our passion for the environment.

It may be ironic, but laundry detergent is dirty. Traditionally consisting of roughly 80 percent water, detergent winds up causing a lot of waste and environmental harm. Not only do manufacturers have to use a lot of water to produce it, but it takes a lot of water to package it, and retailers burn a lot of fuel transporting it to their stores. Everybody loses, including the consumer, who has to lug around all those twenty-pound bottles. Bad for the environment and bad for the consumer, the laundry jug is the SUV of the consumer products industry. So we set our sights on the category soon after founding Method.

Concentrated laundry detergent wasn't exactly a new idea. Others had tried it in the United States without much commercial success, and it's the industry standard in space-constrained cultures like Japan. But when we debuted our triple-concentrated formula at Target in August 2004, something clicked. Shoppers warmed to the idea of less pollution and a smaller, lighter bottle. Competitors took note.

Here's where things got interesting. Instead of clogging up the category and slowing down innovation with a number of patents, we encouraged competitors to follow our lead. To any established company in any industry, the practice of not protecting intellectual property would seem like sheer lunacy. Of course, there's a method to the madness. It would be counter to our philosophy to hoard technologies to ourselves. We have a culture that's not afraid to say, "We made a better product, and everybody copied us, so let's go do it again!" OK, maybe that's a weird philosophy, but if we force our competitors to get greener, we are amplifying the positive impact of our business.

Just sixteen months after we launched our concentrated detergent, competitors started coming out with concentrated formulas of their own. All Small & Mighty—a 3x formula—was the first to follow. (Note: A few years later, the folks at Unilever asked to meet with us. Apparently, our 3x launch helped them get board approval to move forward with All Small & Mighty, and they were interested in working together on future category innovation.) By demonstrating the mainstream viability of concentrated detergent, we were provoking the entire industry to change for the better. At this point, most other CPG companies would be saying, "Hey, you guys stole our idea!" Not us. We were thrilled!

Soon Walmart was giving the category a closer look. After examining our business proposition during a short-lived and unsuccessful trial of our detergent, the world's biggest retailer took action. In 2007 Walmart announced that it would sell *only* concentrated detergents beginning in May 2008. (After some griping, even Tide agreed to go along with the plan—though the brand drew the line at 2x).

Walmart's press release on the decision, titled "Can Laundry Detergent Save the Planet?" looked eerily similar to some of the research we had done, noting that if the entire category went to 2x, annual savings in the United States would amount to 400 million gallons of water, 95 million pounds of plastic, and 125 million pounds of cardboard (our numbers were 400 million gallons of water, 85 million pounds of plastic, and enough fuel to run twenty-five thousand cars for a year).

Imitation? Sure, but the facts are the facts. It's just another example of Method's model, which encourages people to follow us so we can innovate again. Whether we talk about laundry, wipes, or toilet-bowl cleaner as examples of good product development or putting our sustainability principles to work, they all attempt to answer the same question: How can we use our business to

▲ **THE DIRTY LITTLE SECRET OF OVERDOSING.** Oversized and confusing caps lead most consumers to use too much detergent, which is bad for your clothes, your skin, your machines, and your planet.

create the kind of positive change that ripples throughout the industry and multiplies our positive impact?

Our goal is to stay ahead of the game. While our competitors continue to push back on ultra-concentrated detergents, in 2010 Method launched the first ever 8x concentrated detergent. Your move, Tide.

Of course, you can't always count on your competitors following your lead—especially if they've got a different kind of "green" in mind. For this next example, we recommend looking up a 2010 article in the *Wall Street Journal* by reporter Ellen Byron called "The Great American Soap Overdose." Byron examines America's addiction to laundry detergent, asking why laundry detergent doses are so confusing—why the fill lines are so hard to read and why the caps are oversized.

These are good questions. The crux of our problem with overdosing comes down to the size of the caps. The average detergent cap is more than twice the size required to wash a full load (and the "natural" brands are just as guilty as the rest). Detergent manufacturers are quick to point out that they're against overdosing and that they're constantly looking for ways to curb it. Right. Billions of dollars and a century of R&D, and you can't design a better cap? We don't buy it. This kind of "we're on your side" rhetoric is symbolic of a greater ideological battle in sustainable business today. It's a fight between those who want to *appear* green as they serve their business interests and defend the status quo against those who are willing to invest in creating better, greener solutions that will help people live more sustainably.

Detergent manufacturers argue that they've left dosing instructions vague because consumers want control, and specific dosing instructions would pin them in. We wish we could tell you we're kidding. Sure, the consumer is boss, but since when does that justify a cavernous cap that makes you *feel* as though you're using too little even when you stop at the recommended amount? If detergent manufacturers were truly concerned about the negative effects of using too much of their product, they would reduce the size of their caps to correspond to the amount needed for a heavy load. Half cap, half load—simple enough, right? That's what Method did when we launched our first laundry detergent in 2004. Boom, problem solved. Furthermore, given the huge volume of laundry detergent sold every year, right-sizing the cap would save manufacturers millions in plastic costs and create an enormous sustainability benefit. But no. The big brands keep selling oversize caps, counting on consumers to overuse the product and buy more.

Tired of the cap game altogether, we launched our 8x concentrated detergent with a pump dispenser rather than a cap. That's right, no cap at all. The

method®
sustainability initiatives

method's entire line of home care and personal care products are non-toxic, made with naturally derived, biodegradable ingredients that are tough on dirt and easy on the planet.

PRODUCTS

transparency

we believe in transparency so we disclose all our ingredients.

recycled plastic

we make recyclable bottles from 100% recycled plastic resulting in zero waste and a 70% lower carbon footprint.

Cradle to Cradle®

we are proud to offer the first range of certified Cradle to Cradle® cleaning products.

ingredient safety

we're recognized by EPA's Design for the Environment (DfE) program for the ingredient safety of over 50 products.

EPEA-assessed

we have all of our materials assessed by the EPEA for health and environmental safety.

PROCESS

biodiesel fleet

the majority of our customer shipments in california and the northeast are via biodiesel truck.

reduction incentives

we offer incentives to suppliers to reduce carbon emissions and ultimately lower our impact.

greensourcing program

we have a supplier sustainability program that drives green innovation.

fuel efficiency

our domestic shipments are done with an EPA SmartWay Transport member freight company for better fuel efficiency.

COMPANY

climate-sensitive

as a climate-sensitive business, we offset the carbon emissions from our manufacturing, travel and office use.

B corporation

we are a founding B Corporation business and use the power of purpose-driven private enterprise to create social and environmental change.

Cradle to Cradle®

we are a Cradle to Cradle® business recognized for our environmental product design and green business leadership.

never tested on animals

we were PETA's 2006 company of the year and are certified cruelty-free for our no-animal testing policy.

LEED-certified

our san francisco HQ is a LEED-certified green building.

great cleaning comes naturally to us. find out more at **methodhome.com** innovation turns a cumbersome, messy, two-handed process into a simple, one-handed squirt. It still gives the consumer control, and it drastically reduces both the incidence and magnitude of overdosing. If you want to use a little more, that's up to you—but an extra squirt is 16 percent more, not double or triple what you need!

The reason for this is simple math. Method recently conducted a study that concluded that 53 percent of detergent consumers "eyeball it" or use a full cap, which is about double the recommended dose. This is the dirty little secret of the laundry business, and every manufacturer knows it. If half of all consumers use double what they need, then 33 percent of all laundry detergent purchased in America is unnecessary waste. Millions and millions of pounds of excess soap down the drain. Bad for the environment, but good for big brands' shareholders. Consider that more than $3 billion of laundry detergent is sold each year in America. If a third of that is pure waste, it's safe to assume that detergent manufacturers make about $1 billion a year on consumers overusing laundry detergent. It's clearly not that the technology to make caps less wasteful and easier to use has eluded detergent manufacturers all these years—they have a billion little reasons not to look for it in the first place.

At this point, you might be saying to yourself, *Isn't it just laundry detergent? Is it really that big a deal?* Well, don't listen to us. Follow the water. Consider that 1,100 loads of laundry are started every second in America. That means approximately 100 million pounds of laundry detergent go down the drain and into our waterways every year. Still not impressed? Take a field trip to your local water treatment plant and ask an engineer what all that soap is doing to your local ecosystem (not to mention your drinking water). Design has the power to change our world for the better, but only if we use it for good. Sometimes that's as simple as redesigning the cap. It boils down to linking the average consumer's interest in "control" and "mess-free" detergent with the social and environmental interest of limiting overdosing—in effect, aligning selfishness with selflessness.

MAKING IT SELFISH . . . FOR OUR STAKEHOLDERS

When it comes to shareholders and sustainability, most companies prefer to contribute to green charities rather than make substantive changes in areas like production and shipping. After all, shareholders are generally looking for efficiencies, not sustainable practices. Throw in a bit of charity and everyone feels better. It doesn't have to be this way. You can inspire your stakeholders to *want* greener practices—and you can even give up the charity in the process. At least, that's how we work.

Few companies devote as many resources to causes as we do, but unlike those businesses that devote a preset percentage of profits to green charities, we push almost everything back into the business and share our people instead. In doing this, we're acting with Gandhi's words in mind—"Be the change you want to see in the world." The change we want to see is not companies giving away their profits, but businesses truly creating good, so that, as they grow, so too does their positive impact on the world. We want to see businesses in which all employees are engaged meaningfully in causes that matter to them and relate to the role that business plays in making the world greener and safer.

Take Patagonia, a pioneer in sustainable business. Its founder, Yvon Chouinard, is a true hero for entrepreneurs like us—someone who's been able to build a business that truly aligns social and environmental interest with the bottom line. If we could do half of what it does to produce positive environmental impact, we'd be doing well. But we have a difference of opinion in our model. Patagonia practices what we call the steal-and-donate model, wherein a large portion of profits are taken from the business and given to nonprofits. It's a worthy pursuit, but we don't like the inherent assumption that business is bad, and so investments are better made elsewhere. If the intention of a business is to create positive benefit and it's truly committed to progress, we think it's better to invest the profits back into growing and innovating, and use the *people* in that business to invest in the community through time and participation. To limit our growth is to limit our impact.

We try to align our deep green values with the interests of our shareholders and our company as a whole. One of the ways we've done this is by being recognized as a B corporation (or benefit corporation), something of a gold star in the green industry. The B corporation is a new corporate form that attempts to generate profits while advancing and maintaining social and environmental benefits. B corporations may seek to address climate change, health problems, or poverty, but they do so by being both profitable and competitive. B Lab, the organization that certifies all B corporations, audits and certifies the environmental and social practices of a company and publishes them online in a completely transparent way, providing a real-time, public sustainability report for each B corporation. Beyond real-time sustainability and corporate responsibility reporting, Method has actually changed its Articles of Incorporation to expand the fiduciary duty of the officers of the company to include social and environmental stakeholders. It's not simply "triple bottom line"; it binds us legally to the ethics we espouse, assuring shareholders that the environment and social conditions are considered in every decision we make.

In addition to our B corporation distinction, Method was one of the first companies to be recognized as a cradle-to-cradle company. The theory behind the cradle-to-cradle idea, mentioned earlier in this chapter, is pretty simple. We all know that we can't consume resources infinitely on a finite planet. Too many people creating too much waste, right? Cradle-to-cradle designers begin with the assumption that our problem is not necessarily that there are too many of us or that we consume too much (which in some cases may also be true), but that what we consume is not designed properly.

Cradle-to-cradle designers assert that it's OK to use highly technical materials—after all, they're products of human ingenuity and creativity—as long as we keep them in closed-loop "technical cycles" so those materials are recycled infinitely over and over again. Natural materials should likewise be cycled through a closed-loop biological cycle. Any material that gets introduced to the biological cycle—like the detergent that goes down the drain or the spray cleaner that drifts into the air—should be designed to be compatible with, or better yet, degradable in the natural environment.

What's so inspiring and so important about cradle-to-cradle methodology is that it calls for a positive vision for a future in which people can enjoy an enhanced quality of life *and* environmental and social sustainability. It reconciles the long-standing trade-off between being green and living with abundance and joy. Cradle to cradle is about redesigning the stuff that we consume so that it's good. If you do that, then making and using wonderful things that make us happy becomes a good thing, not something we need to feel guilty about. This is a philosophy we apply to every Method product and to the business itself—something all of us, including our shareholders, are proud of.

MAKING IT SELFISH . . . FOR OUR VENDORS AND PARTNERS

When you're competing with billion-dollar brands, you've got to get creative. Because Method doesn't have the promise of a lot of volume for leverage, we can't appeal to our vendors based on the size of our business alone. To do so, we often employ a guinea pig strategy, wherein we will be the first to take a new technology to market, developing it with a partner, but then we *don't* hold it exclusively for ourselves. Instead, we let that vendor develop it in order to attract other business, even from our competitors. This tactic allows us to get to market more quickly, and it allows that vendor to gain new business by building capability in a new area. It aligns our interest in gaining access to new technologies with the vendor's interest in business development. As a result, Method becomes a lightning rod for new ideas and technology. And as long as we can continue to be the fastest, we maintain our competitive advantage.

If the fastest path to sustainability in the supply chain is aligning your interests with those of your vendors, then it's critical not only to understand your own business, but theirs, as well. That's why making it selfish for your vendors can't happen without what we call blue-collar sustainability.

Building true sustainability into a business is a blue-collar job. While the slick press releases and shiny solar panels might catch people's attention, creating real environmental wins and healthier products is a roll-your-sleeves-up, knock-down, drag-out kind of job.

That's because sustainable product design is about redesigning, dematerializing, digging, and never taking "It can't be done" as an answer. This can't be done without understanding where something comes from and where it goes, something that requires considerable time at the source and the dump. At Method, we pride ourselves on fighting the good fight where it matters, on the front lines—in the factories and fields and recycling centers. We often find that the biggest sustainability wins come from the most unexpected places.

When you innovate with green materials, you often encounter barriers you didn't know existed. This was the case when, after years of work to develop a postconsumer recycled (PCR) plastic that was clear enough to meet Method standards, we tried to start making it into bottles. How would we ensure that our special, proprietary PCR resin never got mixed up with ordinary virgin resin? The only solution was to build our own resin silo (think silo on a farm) to house it. So down to Kentucky we went to visit the bottle plant.

Ultimately, being able to make bottles out of 100 percent PCR resin meant using a crane to install a silo upright outside the bottle factory, installing the pipes and hoses to get the raw material into the building, and writing detailed quality-assurance specifications to make sure it was being processed correctly. It meant tracking the transport specifications to make sure the proper equipment would be on hand to load the silo. It wasn't glamorous work, but it was necessary work. And now the bottles we make have a drastically lower carbon footprint—60 percent lower, in fact—due to that work done on the front lines. Meanwhile our vendor has become the world leader in high-quality, 100 percent recycled packaging.

Similar challenges have revealed themselves with every earnest effort we've made to green our business or our products. Converting our trucks to biodiesel meant negotiating warranties with truck manufacturers who wanted to void them because we were going to run them on waste vegetable oil. Getting our distribution center running on solar energy required bolting the panels to decommissioned truck trailers and running weatherized wiring into the building from the outside. Reducing our energy use had us installing insulation around our mixing tanks.

Rolling up your sleeves is the only real way to create more sustainable product. Poking around in garbage cans, factories, and fields is the only way to truly understand a product's impact and to overcome the abstraction that makes designing sustainability from the ivory tower so easy but so misguided.

We also make it selfish for our retailers. Through ten years of practice, Method has gained much knowledge of what works and what doesn't in trying to build sustainability into business. Retailers are often looking for ways to go green, but most have been around for a while and have certain ways of doing things. That's where a more consultative approach to working with customers (rather than just a sales approach) pays dividends. By working with, understanding, and truly helping retailers to capitalize on the changing category trends and consumer sentiments, we are able to establish a deeper relationship. At Target, for example, our business relationship now includes interfaces with the sus-

▲ **BIODIESEL IS HOW WE ROLL.** The majority of our products are delivered with veggie oil instead of dirty fossil fuels.

tainability team, the marketing teams, the consumer insights people, and the supply chain, in addition to the traditional buyer relationship. By providing insights and working collaboratively with multiple functions within Target, ideas cross-pollinate and get built upon, which builds shared ownership. As a result, ideas have a greater chance of seeing the light of day, and Method's strategic value is elevated. In becoming a resource for our retailers, we connect ourselves with them in both profit and purpose. It might be uncommon to have a greenskeeper at a sales call, but the next time a competitor comes, check in hand, to buy your shelf space away, that retailer will remember the invaluable knowledge you bring.

A MODEL FOR CHANGE: PERFECT AS THE ENEMY OF GOOD

A lot of companies talk about "the pursuit of perfection," but our mantra is "Be the best at getting better." The reasoning here is simple: If you're hung up on releasing the perfect product or message, you'll spend too much time perfecting behind the scenes and not enough time advancing in the market. Nowhere has this been truer than in our push toward sustainable formulas and packaging. We've learned that you can't force the perfect design solution. It doesn't happen. You have to employ a series of imperfect solutions and then be the best at getting better.

Imperfect solutions? The big brands hate ideas like this, but it's exactly how we've been able to out-innovate our competitors. Take our refill pouches. Years ago, we sold refill containers of soap in large recyclable bottles. Problem was, while they were recyclable and used less plastic than another starter unit, they still used a lot of plastic—much of which ends up in landfills. Instead of banging our heads against the wall in search of a perfect solution, our employees created a refill pouch, made from just 16 percent as much plastic as the bottle. Because of its multilayer design, the pouch can't be recycled (yet), but the net effect is less plastic in landfills. It wasn't a popular move with our dark green advocates at first, but when they did the math, they understood that it was a lot better for the environment, and they got on board. Although imperfect, this format now gives us leverage to motivate our vendors to crack the code on how to make it recyclable. And in the meantime we partnered with Teracycle so that the pouches can be upcycled into new products such as killer looking bags.

We think too many people and companies are obsessed with claiming perfection. Sustainable this, green that—it's all a little hard to believe. Method's not

▲ PROGRESS, NOT PERFECTION.
While this refill is not the perfect solution,
it puts us on the path to reach perfection.
(Psst: and now we take them back and
recycle them into bags.)

a sustainable business; no business is truly 100 percent sustainable . . . yet. But we realize that our company, like each of us as individuals, is a work in progress. We must be the change we seek, so we put the onus on ourselves to make healthier, happier homes. As a business, we want to be sustainable, but our goal is not just sustainability. As our friend Michael Braungart says about marriage, who wants the relationship with one's spouse to be merely sustainable? Nobody! We all want rich and fulfilling relationships that add value and meaning to our lives. You get out what you put in, and we feel the same way about business. Sustainability in the green movement is the same—good enough for now but just the beginning of something much better.

After all, it's why we're in business: to change business. We started Method with a deep desire to create change for the better. Good policy alone is not enough—Adam learned as much working on the Kyoto Protocol, which was undermined by the interests of traditional business. Time for a one-eighty. Time to use business as a positive force, as an agent of positive change. But to do so, business itself must be redesigned. This doesn't have to be painful; we believe inspiration is a better tool for change than shame. And the best way to inspire people is with super-cool products that present simple solutions.

Method is a solution, but it's only one solution. We need others, but for now, we will do our part to provide solutions to those who want to live cleanly, greenly, and most important, pleasurably and optimistically. Traditional environmentalism chastises the very people it wants to change. Doom and gloom, shame and blame. It's been around for thirty years, and no wonder it doesn't work. Don't get us wrong: Environmentally speaking, things are bad—really bad. And we've got to do something about it *now*. But we have two choices: Sit around and analyze the problem and debate its minutiae, arguing that this is better than that, or get off our collective asses and *do something* about it. We've chosen the latter.

That's why it's progress, not perfection, that drives us. If the perfect solution to our environmental crises was evident, we would have found it by now. The challenge, and our opportunity, is to make change in an imperfect and resistive environment and move toward better solutions.

With respect to sustainability, we don't ask, Are we there yet? We know that the answer to that question is no, and it will be for a while. Instead, we ask, Are we as close as we can be? What can we do to be closer? We think those are more powerful questions, because they compel us to act, to make change, to do something. As T. S. Eliot wrote, "Between the motion / And the act / Falls the Shadow." Rhetoric doesn't create solutions; action does.

ERROR AUTOPSY: WIPEOUT

The idea of launching wipes never sat well with us. Like its cousin, the paper towel, the wipe is a convenient form of everyday domestic life, but in exchange for saving seconds in the kitchen, they spend lifetimes in a landfill. Unfortunately, this product form is not going away anytime soon, so we figured that if consumers are going to insist on using wipes, let's at least give them a better one. When first launched, our cleaning wipes were in a plastic hourglass-shaped canister. All the parts were recyclable, but there was a big footprint because of all the material in the packaging. With natural, compostable cloths and a biodegradable cleaning formula, they were better for the environment than the mainstream alternative. So we set out to make them even better for the environment. Or so we thought. Our solution was to replace the canister with a flat pack, like that in which baby wipes are normally packaged.

Care to guess which one's greener? Technically, it's the flatpak. The benefits of using a lot less packaging far outweigh the benefits of using recycled plastic.

ORIGINAL HOURGLASS CONTAINER

VS.

NEW FLATPAK CONTAINER

PAST

 postconsumer recycled resin

PRESENT

🖓 lots of plastic

FUTURE

👍 easily and commonly recycled

PAST

 can't employ recycled plastic

PRESENT

 one-eighth as much material

FUTURE

 not commonly recycled because it's multilayered

But you have to bring people along with you . . . and this time we didn't. Some customers were confused about how the flatpak was supposed to work. Others just liked the hourglass container more. Many overlooked the new version altogether, searching for the hourglass container. The result: flatpaks flatlined, and our sales plummeted.

Because of lessons like this, we don't decide what materials to use based only on what makes the most positive impact initially; we look at the qualitative layer too. How cool is it? Will people buy it? Will it tell a story? Every change is a judgment call. There's an inextricable link between the benefit from a scientific standpoint and the benefit from an emotional standpoint. Say a decision might improve our environmental impact by ten "points," but the consumer will think it's really lame, or worse yet won't buy it at all. Then we're considering another decision that's not quite as green—say it improves our footprint by eight points—but it's really intuitive and engaging and makes adopting that innovation more simple or fun. Just as in the European refilling stations versus refills example described earlier, we're going to pick the eight, because our goal is not ten, it's ten thousand. Our goal is not to have an incrementally better product that never sees the light of day. Our goal is to move an entire industry to a more sustainable place, and that takes more than one step. There is no point in making a greener product if nobody uses it.

One small change sparks exponential growth. Be committed to the next innovation, not the current one.

OUR GREEN GIANT MUSE: GARY HIRSHBERG, STONYFIELD FARM

If we're Jedi, Gary Hirshberg is our Yoda. And if you're a yogurt fan, then you're probably a lover of Stonyfield Farm. Gary has been at the forefront of transformational environmental and social movements for thirty years. From his early days as an educator and activist to his current position as president and CE-Yo of Stonyfield Farm, the world's largest organic yogurt company, Hirshberg's positive outlook has inspired countless followers to help make the world around them better. Arguably, no one else can take more credit for bringing organic to the masses than Gary.

So what have we stolen from Gary? Two things. First, the belief that you can blend purpose and profits. Gary has consistently reinforced our confidence that doing good in the world and being good at business aren't mutually exclusive. One of his company's five missions is "to serve as a model that environmentally and socially responsible businesses can also be profitable," and Gary realizes this vision in every aspect of his company. He is one of the masters and legends of infusing mission and purpose into the heart and soul of business. While staying true to a very serious mission, he has proved that the best way to introduce the masses to organic choices is through a fun and engaging brand (and a lot of yummy flavors, naturally).

To Gary, blending purpose and profits doesn't mean compromising one or the other. With each consumer he convinces to switch to organic (growing his

▲ OUR GREEN GIANT MUSE.
Gary Hirschberg is the master of
blending purpose and profits without
compromising one or the other.

business), he benefits the planet and human health (advancing his mission). It
hasn't been easy, though. Gary made some tough decisions to get where he is—
perhaps most famously the choice to sell in Walmart, which ruffled a lot of feath-
ers in the organic industry. But as he'll tell you, if you want to catch a fish, you
need to fish where the fish are. Meanwhile, taking organic big has had a ripple
effect, pushing other large companies, like Kraft, to expand their organic offer-
ings (much as we've been pushing companies like P&G to remove petrochemi-
cals from their products). As Gary puts it, "The only way to influence the
powerful forces in this industry is to become a powerful force."

The second thing we've stolen from Gary is his mentorship style. Gary took
the time to meet with us during the early years—an enormous act of generosity,
considering his busy schedule and the fact that we were just two kids starting a
soap company. As we soon learned, that's just Gary—he has always been committed to mentoring younger, socially minded entrepreneurs by helping them
navigate the early years of birthing a business. And we've learned something
profound from that example: You can make a far greater impact on the world by
inspiring like-minded entrepreneurs than by simply growing your own business.
In fact, Gary's efforts to help the next generation of business leaders were a big
part of why we wrote this book. Thanks, Gary!

obsession

4

KICK ASS
AT FAST

**if you're not the biggest,
you'd better be the fastest**

It's not the big that eat the small, it's the fast that eat the slow.

—Jason Jennings and Laurence Haughton

THANKS TO THE BLINDING PACE OF MODERN TECH-
nology and real-time data, we live and work in an anything, anywhere, anytime media-driven market. A flatscreen in every room, a smartphone in
every pocket, and ever-shrinking microchips anywhere we can fit them. Amid the
media mania, it's easy to forget that the rise in rapid technology is just a symp-
tom of something deeper: our society's insatiable demand for speed.

Take a (quick) look around. Soaring consumer demand for the latest and
greatest innovations and gadgets; aggressive retailing strategies devised to
move the largest volumes of product at the lowest margins possible; impatient
investors infatuated with quarterly returns, month-over-month sales reports,
and up-to-the-second statistical analyses—our blind need for speed has become a driving force in every segment of the economy. And no wonder! No matter if you're buying, selling, or investing, in today's marketplace, he who is fastest
is often first.

But while speed is great for the fast-paced consumer, it's a blessing and a
curse for business. Whereas past business leaders had no choice but to take a
wait-and-see approach upon implementing any important decision, modern
entrepreneurs can launch today and collapse tomorrow. Success and failure

come quickly. Commitment is fleeting. Multi-million-dollar network television shows are canceled after a single episode with bad ratings. National political campaigns implode after one insensitive sound bite goes viral and leads to a bad week in the polls. But the same is true for companies like ours that rely on brand and consumer approval to last. In a world where consumers are bombarded by thousands of products per second, brand loyalty is a fleeting thing.

The overwhelming demand for what we want right now has become a self-propagating trend. Products are updated, relaunched, and rebranded even when there is no substantive change—all in an effort to capture consumers' attention and remain relevant. Electronics companies engineer smartphones and computers that boast the most recent technology but will be outdated in a matter of months. Sports fans can buy limited-edition bags of potato chips emblazoned with images of league champions within days of the Super Bowl or World Series. All this planned obsolescence not only makes it increasingly difficult to stay ahead; it also generates a massive waste problem. E-waste from the ubiquitous growth of computers, phones, and electronics accounts for 50 million tons of trash each year, the equivalent of a hundred thousand fully loaded 747s.

Even the notoriously slow-to-evolve publishing industry has been picking up the pace. Downloading books with the touch of a button, one in ten Americans now curl up with a Kindle, Nook, or Sony e-reader rather than a printed book. And the medium isn't the only thing evolving, either. The consumer's demand for speed is spurring popular brand-name authors, like James Patterson (*Along Came a Spider*) and Jack Canfield (*Chicken Soup for the Soul*), to crank out ten or twenty new books every year (with a good deal of help from their coauthors). Anywhere you look in today's consumer market, consumers reward brands in a hurry.

Famous for moving large volumes of product at low prices, or "stacking it high and watching it fly," the retail industry understands the breakneck pace of modern commerce as well as any. Good retail is fast by nature, but the pace at which new products come and go in today's marketplace is unprecedented. By now, most of us have probably suffered the experience of discovering that our favorite flavor, scent, or style of any given product—or sometimes the product itself—has been discontinued. Fewer than one in seven new products in the average grocery store gains enough traction to survive its first year. This kind of pressure to succeed not only stifles new product development, but also forces brands and retailers alike down a one-way path toward diminishing returns by way of smaller and smaller margins on larger and larger volumes of goods.

Consumers and retailers aren't the only ones hooked on speed. Impatient investors analyze Wall Street's every last twitch down to fractions of a cent with split-second accuracy. The impact on commerce is clear: companies in every industry are under pressure to grow faster and create disruptive growth in less time. But when everyone's fast, it's no longer enough to be just fast. Fast is not an exceptional quality; it's par for the course. And when you're small, being faster than your competitors is your biggest—and sometimes only—advantage.

Ever since we founded Method, we've used speed to trump size. What choice did we have? Unilever, P&G—some of the first multinationals in the world—were soap companies, and it took them over a century to grow to the size they are today. Rather than invite competition, they've learned they're powerful enough to define the rules of the game to their advantage, designing a game of scale that few are able to play. Our competitors invest heavily in keeping upstarts like us from joining the party in the first place. (Don't believe us? Try to get an inch of shelf space at a national grocery chain—a process we'll discuss more in the next chapter.) Even when we reached $100 million in revenue, we were still more than five hundred times smaller than the leaders of our industry. Racing innovations to market and taking on added risks are the only ways a smaller company like ours can stay ahead of leading consumer trends and outpace slower-moving industry giants. Our strategy is "running between the legs of Goliath." We may be small and squirrelly, but we're quick on our feet!

We know most entrepreneurs understand how important it is to be fast; we want to change the world (or at least make a buck) in a hurry, and we realize that if we dillydally, someone else will beat us to it. Every entrepreneur we know has

---

SLOW REVOLUTION

In a world that is moving too fast, it's no surprise to see the gradual introduction of *slow* as a winning strategy. In the words of George Jetson, "Jane! Get me off this crazy thing!"

In 1986 Carlo Petrini launched the slow-food movement, advocating local food prepared with care and savored without haste. Today, his organization claims a hundred thousand members in 132 countries.

In 2010 in an effort to recapture the coffeehouse experience it was founded on, Starbucks directed its baristas to make no more than two drinks at a time. Customers said the process had begun to feel like being on a conveyer belt.

---

that same impatient itch to create, build, and expand. Speed is a deep-seated part of our DNA—so much so that, if you're like us, you shudder at phrases like "slow build." (Ugh.)

That's why, from day one, we were committed to making Method go as fast as we could. We were paranoid—convinced that, while our style-and-substance approach was unique, if it were successful, it could be copied, and the only thing that could keep us ahead was getting better at being faster in order to outrun our bigger competitors. So while some businesses stick to organic growth—gradually expanding as sales allow—we decided to pursue outside capital and get off the ground as quickly as possible. We wanted to go big or go home.

In the months after launch, we constantly updated our PowerPoint presentations to show any and all top-line growth, including every metric we could think of to encourage our investors to keep their faith alive. To no one's surprise, skeptical retail partners paid a lot more attention to us once we could demonstrate quick growth. (Nothing beats kicking off a pitch meeting with a hockey-stick sales chart that promises fast-growing sales.) Demonstrating 300 percent growth in less than a quarter by aggressively driving distribution and expanding our product line not only gave us credibility, it also created an aura of excite-

▲ SMALL + SPEED = SUCCESS. SMALL + SLOW = ROADKILL.
Thanks to Method alumnus Tom Fishburne for the cartoon!

ment. Retailers weren't the only ones calling us back. Investors, job seekers, journalists—our rapid growth made everything easier, from establishing new relationships with manufacturers to hiring eager new employees. Of course, growth is like an addictive drug: After each new high, it takes more and more to keep you flying. But as we quickly learned, rapid growth has a way of hiding your problems.

No matter what industry you are in or what kinds of customers you serve, you're constantly told that speed is the surest way to win. And it's true—at least in the short-term. In fact this obsession was originally just called "speed." Over time, however, we discovered that truly "kicking ass at fast" (as opposed to simply being fast at growing) required a balance of long-term vision and short-term agility. Easier said than done.

BALANCING ACTS

In a business environment increasingly defined by short-term goals, quick fixes, and overnight success stories, winning in the short term can appear to be all that matters. But being the fastest and the first can cut both ways. While the benefits of speed are sweet, the consequences when it goes awry are sobering and significant. Speed causes mistakes—and at high speed, even the tiniest mistake can have catastrophic consequences. Rushed research can be sloppy, incomplete, or misinterpreted. Hurried testing overlooks errors and missteps. Careless launches let down your partners, retailers, and customers. It took us a long time and a lot of mistakes to understand this.

In the beginning, being fast—fast to prototype, fast to test, fast to market— was key to our survival; we had to prove we were here to stay. But we've learned over the years that speed doesn't always translate directly into success. Without wisdom, speed is recklessness.

In business, we tend to think about *fast* in terms of all the old clichés. Fast talk, fast food, fast living—in the wrong context, *fast* has a bad reputation. To be sure, this kind of fast has its place. We've sprinted through our share of corporate objectives, aiming for short-term sales over substance. But an obsession with this kind of fast won't get the best results. It'll get you an ulcer. Hence, of the seven obsessions in this book, none is as prone to misinterpretation as kicking ass at fast. That's why we've devoted much of this chapter to distinguishing the right kind of fast (and avoiding speed for speed's sake).

THE HAZARDS OF FAST

To say we had a tendency to grow too fast too early is something of an understatement. We sped, we raced, and we overreached. Now, it wouldn't be accurate to say we were reckless; we were just fighting gravity. The realities of getting a start-up off the ground demand explosive growth and strong momentum to build support. It takes three times as much energy to get something moving as it does to maintain momentum. In fact, as near as we can tell, there is no such thing as growing too fast when you're a brand-new company. But four years in, when we started exploring new areas solely because of the growth opportunities available to us . . . that was our biggest mistake. We started moving into new product categories simply because we could.

The best example of this was in 2003, when Walmart expressed interest in selling our hand wash but told us the concept would be more interesting if we also had body wash. We were hearing the same desire from other retailers, who were excited about the success of our new hand wash and therefore eager to see us launch companion products.

Building a business is like building a house—you must have a good foundation. And when we laid the foundation for Method, we never intended to build a body-care addition. Working with the world's largest retailers to create a body wash was our first major leap away from home care (a category we'd grown to know well). It was like adding a room on the third story of your house . . . without anything beneath it. We let the business guide the brand, instead of letting the brand guide the business. While the economics were really attractive, a Method body wash product didn't make sense strategically.

But we did it anyway, and it backfired for several reasons. We rushed the product to market and spread our marketing dollars too thin to properly support it—but these were merely tactical errors. One of the strategic keys to our success up until then had been taking a personal-care approach to home care, which was disruptive. But with body wash, we were taking a personal-care approach to personal care. It lacked any disruptive point of view! More important, we were simply pursuing a business opportunity, a deviation from our tried-and-true method of exploiting a cultural shift.

Right about the time we were getting distracted with body wash, we also launched Vroom—a parallel brand devoted to car-care goods. This time, it was Target that felt there was an opportunity for our brand—and we agreed, though we believed auto-care products would be better suited to a new brand, hence

▲ **SPEED KILLS.** You will overreach at some point but do your best to resist the urge. More companies die by growing too quickly than too slowly.

Vroom. Never heard of it? Probably because we sold it shortly after launch. After these and a number of similar mistakes, we realized that in our rush to be the fastest, we were often slowing ourselves down. We were spending more time correcting minor quality problems (leaky bottles, faulty pumps) and major screw-ups than we were making our core products better.

And therein lies the problem: Inherently, speed comes with a lot of risks—more, in fact, than any of our other obsessions. Yet the rewards of moving quickly usually go hand in hand with the dangers, and shorter development cycles allow for more opportunities. In the early stages of launching a business, speed is your friend, but mishandled, it can become a liability. One of our biggest lessons over the last ten years has been figuring out when to step on the gas and when to hit the brakes. Learning to go fast is one thing, but learning to *kick ass* at high speed takes experience and maturity. So how do you walk that balance between long-term thinking and short-term innovation and speed? It's a question that strikes the heart of this obsession.

DEVELOPING AGILITY

Inspiration may come quickly, but innovation takes time. Some ideas take off fast, spreading through the world like wildfire. But the most successful ideas are those with real depth and relevance—ones with staying power. You can see this distinction in the music industry all the time. Shallow pop songs catch fire fast ("Ice, Ice, Baby!") and die just as quickly. Sometimes not fast enough. Meanwhile, the artists with soul and resonance—Eric Clapton, the Rolling Stones, Aretha Franklin—may initially take longer to catch on, but they're the ones who find their way into our hearts year after year. For Method, our challenge is to find that balance between a long-term vision with depth and catchy, short-term appeal. It's the difference between having a foundation and being a fad.

Naturally, speed cuts both ways, and as we've grown, we've had to be careful about moving too slowly. Enter agility—a skill that allows you to speed up or slow down when you need to. First, you must know if the clock is on your side. Can you afford to hold off on an opportunity like body wash or Vroom—or do you need to act immediately? A simple way we think about this now is by asking ourselves, "What is more likely to hurt the business: going too slow or going too fast?" This is where having an established point of view is absolutely essential. You want to have an unwavering vision, but incredible flexibility in how you bring it to life. To put it another way, you want to stay true to the destination but be open as to how you get there.

Good branding, for example, takes patience. Sticking to your point of view is essential. Innovation, on the other hand, is about using the brand as a lens to seek out new opportunities. Take a look at two recent success stories in the retail clothing industry, J. Crew and H&M. Over the past few years, J. Crew has revived its brand by resurrecting a clear brand point of view that's highly curated and refined. Fast and innovative? Not really. We all know what next year's J. Crew catalog is going to look like. Established and timeless, the brand has found a consistent recipe for style and success. In contrast, Sweden-based H&M has made its name on fast fashion—bringing the latest, up-to-the minute trends from the pages of *US Weekly* to a store near you in a matter of days or weeks. Speed is its biggest advantage. Unlike J. Crew, H&M innovates so quickly that there is no such thing as an H&M look. H&M is not a brand you wear; it's a brand you shop.

Somewhere between the timeless style of the J. Crew brand and the trend-forward appeal of a leading innovator like H&M is the sweet spot we call agility. For us, agility comes down to recognizing when to pursue an opportunity like partnering with Karim Rashid and when to pass up an opportunity like Vroom. In retrospect, our most agile decisions have been based on equal parts artistic vision (patience) and operational excellence (speed). Striking this balance is not as hard as it sounds, and it's the difference between agility and recklessness. At Method, we've discovered all sorts of new ways to leverage our smaller size and speed in every department to make agile decisions every day and kick ass at fast.

A HEAD WITHOUT A BODY Try as you might, you won't achieve fast results by pushing employees to move faster, cramming your existing business processes into shorter timelines, or rushing your suppliers to meet impossible deadlines. Genuinely speeding up an organization requires fundamentally reshaping how it operates, inside and out. That's why we've built speed into every level of our organization, rethinking every role, process, and department.

One of the best ways we've been able to do this is by insourcing creativity and R&D innovation and outsourcing production. That is to say, we do our own intellectual property work, from graphic design to formulation, and we farm out the direct labor of logistics and manufacturing. We believe creativity should always happen on the inside. It is the soul of your brand—the ideas, designs, formulas, and technologies that give the brand its *specialness*. Those functions that we consider strategic, like buying the highest quality materials, we do in house. For those things that we don't need to do any better than our competitors—say, how efficiently we get our products to stores—we partner with the experts. We're not wasting valuable time and resources in areas where we can't leverage much of a competitive advantage. We're like a head without a body. Building the business on this model is one of the keys to our agility, because we can spend time focusing on the things we're good at while working with people who are great at the things we're clueless about.

The obvious argument for keeping creative work in-house rather than handing it over to outside specialists comes back to authenticity. When your market-

▲ **DON'T OUTSOURCE YOUR SOUL.** One of our green chefs cooking up the next great thing in the office laboratory.

ing team sits at a desk between the industrial design specialists (developing new prototypes) and your customer-care employees (fielding advocates' calls and e-mails), it's inevitable that the branding, labels, and advertising copy they write will come from a genuine place, gelling over time to produce a more consistent and pitch-perfect representation of the brand. Plus, owning all the creative functions yourself means you can not only make changes to the look and feel of the brand quickly and inexpensively, but you also can rapidly integrate everything from new green chemistries to cutting-edge packaging materials.

So why do we outsource production? Because hard assets (factories, fleets of trucks, that office in the south of France) tie up capital and dramatically increase a business's debt load, acting like an anchor on growth. Partnering with vendors allows us to redirect money we would otherwise be spending on machines and real estate to resources that enhance the brand's specialness. It also keeps us nimble, enabling us to work with a wide variety of innovators and find the ideal partner for a new product or concept. To this end, we've developed a diverse network of vendors with a broad range of skills—a portfolio of partners, each with its unique strengths and specialties. We have partners who can precision-print on the complex curves of our hand-wash bottles and others who specialize in volume, labeling a bottle on three different sides 120 times per minute. Whatever idea the head comes up with, we can build the body to match. And when the market changes, demanding a change in how we produce a product, we have the ability to plug in and out of different parts of our manufacturing infrastructure. This high degree of fluidity allows us to be innovative and agile at the same time.

But just because we don't own or operate any factories doesn't mean we're out of touch with what goes on at the production end. Our products are produced in the Midwest, and we've got people on the ground in Chicago working hand in hand with our manufacturing partners to bring everything to life. This is a critically important strategic investment we've made to build manufacturing understanding into our business process even though we don't own or operate the factories. It's a hybrid model. Instead of just throwing the specs over the wall to the manufacturer, we work with our contractor to engineer new solutions on the factory floor. It demonstrates that we have skin in the game, that we're going to roll up our sleeves and help get things done, that we're accountable and we take responsibility for making sure our vision is brought to life.

MAKE FAST FRIENDS It's not that hard to find good suppliers, those that embrace agility as a core value and deliver on it. And once you find them, you can build timelines to ensure that they live up to your idea of speed as a core competency. But other companies already do these kinds of things. To be the fastest, you need to get creative. Be a guinea pig for your vendors; be their marquis client and help them generate new business in return for trying something new with you. In our case, this might be an innovative, difficult-to-fabricate bottle, an expensive and unusual pump, or a new sustainable ingredient. While examples abound, one vendor who really nailed it for us was Amcor, one of the world's largest PET plastic bottle manufacturers. Tasked with making us a bottle entirely from recycled plastic—the world's first—Amcor overcame innumerable technical challenges to succeed. Today, in part as a result of our partnership, Amcor is the industry's leader in recycled PET.

Of course, relying on outside partners means you'll often have to be demanding, but you'll also help them create new capabilities—precisely the kind the market will demand two years down the road. This process allows us to be the first to market with new ideas, and it makes our vendors smarter, more capable, and more competitive. After working for months with a wipes manufacturer to create the world's first completely compostable 100 percent PLA wipe, that

▲ **BE THE GUINEA PIG.** Partnering with one of the world's largest bottle manufacturers to make 100 percent PCR bottles.

manufacturer became the industry's only source for an entirely new technology. (PLA stands for polylactic acid, a class of plastic made from renewable plant materials.)

Today, as a result of this guinea pig approach, every supplier of packaging or raw materials in the CPG industry calls us first with a new idea. We can deliver superior products to market, proving them in the field in the process. We win because our name is on the new technology, and our vendors win because they can show bigger partners (like our competitors) that the new idea works, ultimately selling it to them down the line (which is fine by us). All we ask is that we get the first look at any new technology. Recycled bottles, compostable wipes, natural cleaning solvents—this model has been a winning tactic since the beginning. It's a symbiotic relationship wherein we get first dibs in return for hard work and bringing the innovation to market to prove it works. We are, in effect, our partners' business development lab—a skunk works for the best new ideas in the industry.

ANTICIPATE THE CONSUMER: SET TRENDS, DON'T FOLLOW THEM The world's fastest companies have the ability to quickly and accurately determine the potential for success of a new product, service, or business opportunity. A lot of companies are great at spotting trends or anticipating the next big idea, but few have the ability to quickly vet the idea and determine how to execute it. Frequently the biggest speed bumps and points of derailment for a new idea or innovation are bad use of consumer research.

Consumer research has a tendency to replace actual thinking, and it can stifle real debate and conversations, wasting time in the process. Too frequently, someone will say, "Let's just test it," when they really mean, "I don't have the guts to tell you I don't like your idea, so I'm just going to wait a month and let a group of strangers do it for me."

Extensive research has proven that extensive research is often wrong. As Don Draper, the lead character on *Mad Men*, said, "A new idea is something they don't know yet, so of course it's not going to show up as an option [in consumer research]." When the creators of *Seinfeld* first tested the pilot episode in front of an audience, it famously failed because viewers didn't like the characters and thought Jerry was a weak leading man. As one respondent commented, "You can't get too excited about two guys going to the Laundromat."

Consumer research is more like a rearview mirror than a crystal ball. After all, consumers gravitate to what's most familiar, so listening too closely will leave you with a record of what they've liked in the past. Consumers are great at offering perspectives on products that already exist, but it's your job to spot trends and cultural shifts—like concentrated laundry detergent and sustainable bamboo—before others. Once you find them, it's time to hit the gas.

A different approach to consumer research is needed in order to let big ideas survive the business planning process and keep a company moving fast. For us, it's about being consumer inspired, not consumer led. Being native Detroiters, maybe a Hockeytown analogy will help illustrate this point. Despite being labeled "too small to ever play in the NHL," Wayne Gretzky was the greatest hockey player of all time. Asked why, he said, "Most people skate to where the puck is. I skate to where the puck is going." Our job is to skate to where the consumer is going, and the only way we can do that is to anticipate the direction the consumer is headed. The result is that we give the world something it didn't know it was missing.

In order to grow, you have to have a point of view about the future, and the only way to predict the future is to shape it. Big companies tend to see things the way they are, while entrepreneurs tend to see things the way they could be. Shaping the future requires vision, courage, and regular leaps of faith. At Method, we prefer to integrate consumer insight early in the creative process, using it as a springboard for new ideas to drive innovation. It's one of the reasons we do research in-house. Not only are we better able to anticipate the consumer that way, but we also can do so a lot faster than when we rely on an outside partner that lacks intimacy with the project. Think about it: The more time your in-house experts spend getting used to consumer behavior, the better they get at anticipating how consumers will react in the future and the faster the company can launch new products.

Thanks to the explosion of social and online media, consumer insight is increasingly at your fingertips in real time. Online product reviews, corporate Facebook pages, even your average blog—the Internet offers a wealth of free insights into your brand. While most companies outsource customer service to some cube farm many time zones away, ours reports to the brand team, treating it as consumer insight. By owning the process—listening, consolidating, and putting all those insights into action ourselves—we have a closer, more

▲ **THE METHOD MOMS.** Most of our research is done with our advocates as a form of cocreation.

genuine feel for where things are going every step of the way, allowing us to marry consumer insight with overall strategy and integrate what we learn going forward.

LIVE IN A STATE OF MAKE Living in a state of make is about bringing ideas to life—storyboards, creative materials, campaign concepts, you name it. Perhaps the best way we do this is with prototypes. A prototype is the tangible manifestation of an abstract idea, and it's as useful in helping to suspend disbelief among skeptics as it is in serving as a rough draft for designers to evaluate and evolve. When pitching *Star Wars*, even George Lucas famously prototyped his vision for the film by lying on the ground and acting out scenes with action figures. Building a prototype is a great way to break the navel-gazing cycle of theory and strategy. When dialogue and PowerPoint decks fail to bring about a consensus, a prototype is a low-cost, risk-free means of generating new insights and ensuring everyone is seeing the same vision or movie playing in his head. Once the prototype is finished, each team member can use his or her expertise to figure out how to bring it to life. In the end, this gives everyone the confidence

▲ **LIVE IN A STATE OF MAKE.** Prototype everything to speed up the conversation.

to back the product. Once it's in hand, working backward from a prototype not only ensures that everyone stays focused on the same final product, it means key decision makers (like us) can step away from the project. It's kind of like back in 1960, when Kennedy showed his people at NASA a picture of a man on the moon and told them to make it happen.

Prototyping is key to any decision, so do it early and often. If you were to walk around Method's offices, you'd see prototypes throughout—everything from crude images of bottles and pumps cut and pasted together to refined working concepts of soon-to-launch products. We've even prototyped press clips from the future, mocking up fictional articles that celebrate our vision of success as if it's already been achieved. The idea is to use those physical manifestations to motivate everyone involved and get the feedback (in increasing levels of detail) that we need to take the next step. Like the classic evolutionary chart illustrating our gradual progression from apes, this process can carry a product from the sketch pad to the shelf faster. It's a process that requires a lot of voices and input, but it allows you to put the concept in your hand and accurately assess its potential.

We often simultaneously develop two concepts for the same product, something we call parallel-pathing. Rather than plugging along on a single R&D track—where one team will test and tweak one formula or one package one step at a time—Method will occasionally assign multiple teams to the same task, resulting in several market-ready options. Such was the case with our most recent dish soap, a line launched in 2010. Our developers prototyped two different bottles simultaneously—one, more traditional, with a push-pull cap, and the other, a one-handed pump (like our laundry pump). A lot of companies won't do this because the perception of "wasted resources" makes them uncomfortable. But the reward is speed and flexibility, affording teams more time and more options later in the process. With our dish soap, we had the liberty of finalizing formulas and packages right up until production, making decisions at the eleventh hour without jeopardizing product integrity or our launch date.

FAIL SMALL, FAIL CHEAP There's no better market research than the market. Besting larger rivals often means getting the product to market first, warts and all, and making fixes afterward—a process some of us at Method affectionately refer to as the beta test. Competing in a fast-moving culture and staying ahead of trends is only going to get harder as technology improves and the marketplace opens up to more competition. To stay ahead of bigger brands, tomorrow's entrepreneurs will need to rethink the classic product life cycle. Trends move so fast these days, you can't wait for signs of decline before you start working on the next idea. Forget old clichés like "Don't mess with success" or "If it ain't broke, don't fix it." They're irrelevant.

In order to identify emerging opportunities in a radically changing business environment, there is no better technique than trial and error. This may be why new categories are almost always created in a garage and not at some deep-pocketed big brand. Take our recent hand soap partnership with Disney. Asked to partner with the iconic brand on a Mickey line, we decided to do a beta test. After all, the kids market is incredibly fickle. Dominated by characters like Dora and SpongeBob, it also a graveyard littered with those who've tried and failed. Purchasing decisions shift from the parents to the kids. Could we create something both would love? As this book goes to press, Mickey bottles are reaching

▲ **THE BETA TEST.** Small companies can try many more things per dollar at bat. When you are the little guy you focus on good ideas, prove them, and then scale them up. "Guest Star" is a program where we beta test new fragrance concepts.

a limited selection of retailers. If it bombs, we can withdraw with minimum costs. If it's a hit, you'll be seeing it soon.

We've increasingly tried to use the marketplace to learn, letting sales speak for themselves and creating success through failure. While this approach is faster and less expensive—giving you more at bats per dollar—it requires that you build deeper relationships with your retail clients. After all, you're basically asking them to partner with you on every beta test—for better or worse.

Consider our new "guest star" program, for example, wherein we've set up limited launches of new, trend-forward hand-wash fragrances. These are generally limited to a specific retailer, occasionally within a specific geographical area. While the store categories are usually big, we keep the scope small, and the testing phase rarely lasts longer than a couple of months. How is this different from a test market? you ask. Well, if one of our beta tests is successful and we feel good about the response we're getting, there's no lag—we can instantly ship nationally.

Ultimately, the point of the beta test is to learn about what works and what doesn't. Not only does this keep the cost of failure low, but with each failure, we're able to apply the retrospective lessons to the next test in line, incrementally improving until we have a winning product. It's kind of like hitting a home run fifty feet at a time. Of course, for this approach to be a success, you have to learn how to limit the cost per swing, or you'll burn through capital quickly. In short, fail small and fail cheaply.

SPEED IS A FUNCTION OF CULTURE

> When the rate of change outside exceeds the rate of change inside, the end is in sight.
>
> —Jack Welch

Of course, nobody achieves agility just by outsourcing manufacturing or shipping. As with all our obsessions, kick ass at fast is ultimately a function of our unique culture—the glue that holds everything together. In the early years, we didn't have to make an effort to be inclusive or check in from time to time to be sure everyone was on the same page. We all worked in the same room! (And after work, we all went to the same bar.) Camaraderie flourished, group decision making was second nature, and teamwork never felt like work. In retrospect, our speed as a start-up was just a by-product of our strong culture.

As the company grew, however, our size threatened to slow us down. Weird, right? You'd think that as a start-up builds momentum—adding resources, revenue, experience, and connections—everything would naturally get easier. No more rookie mistakes, no more endless sales pitches and empty cold calls, no more reinventing the wheel with every product launch. The more people you have on board, the more time everyone has to spend getting comfortable with a decision instead of just stepping to the plate and swinging the bat. The challenge—getting people aligned and working together—is no great mystery. And every business book ever published has its own formulas, metaphors, and solutions. Getting everyone on the bus and in the right seat is hard enough, and even when you do, getting them all to agree on where to go and how to get there becomes a daily struggle. For insights into how to stay nimble, we began looking into how *culture* might help speed things up.

Collaboration requires healthy debate. On one hand, we wanted to encourage debate, but drawing the line between debate and dissension can be tough. Quick cultures must have open debate and an environment where people feel safe to share their perspectives, but then such cultures must get people to walk out of the room fully aligned and cognizant of the larger goal at hand. Rapid alignment—getting everyone on the same page—drives great execution, but oftentimes the process of reaching a consensus slows an organization's ability to

"get'er done."
—a mantra often heard within the walls of Method

▲ **SPEED IS A FUNCTION OF CULTURE.** Goliath has a culture of process. We have a culture of speed.

take quick action. So how do you make everyone feel comfortable sharing an opinion while simultaneously aligning behind a single vision?

BE SURE YOUR BRAND HAS A POINT OF VIEW In order to innovate quickly, you need to have a point of view that aligns with your core values. Whenever we assess a new idea or product we're thinking of taking to market, we look at it with a very specific set of criteria in mind: Is it smart? Is it sexy? Is it sustainable? Will it create an advocate? Does it keep Method weird? Ultimately, all of these questions spring from our central mission as a brand: inspiring a happy, healthy home revolution. What's your brand point of view? (If you have to think about this for more than two or three seconds, either you don't have one or you need a better one.) These questions act as filters that speed decision making because they have intuitive meaning and draw from a collective understanding of who we are, what we do, and what our mission is.

Making decisions based on values makes certain that everyone stays focused on what is good for the company, not just for individual careers. Guiding principles drive fast decisions—even (especially) painful ones. A few years ago, after we'd launched a spray air freshener, we discovered that our manufacturer had accidentally contaminated it during production with a common household bacterium. Because we'd used an environmentally friendly preservative (greener, but admittedly weaker), it wasn't strong enough to overcome the bacteria. It sounds kind of scary, but to put it in perspective, the risk of anyone getting sick was lower than that of eating sushi. Although we weren't required to recall the product, and most companies in our position wouldn't have done so, when we considered the issue through the lens of our values, the decision was easy. Within a matter of hours, we started pulling the product from shelves.

When a company does not have a clear POV about its role and how it competes, valuable time is lost considering any tactic or idea that doesn't actually help advance the company's cause. A great POV—informed by our values— helps us stay aligned on who we are and what we do so we can avoid making bad decisions and wasting time by exploring overly broad ideas. For example, we have a clear POV on our typical packaging design: It has to be simple and symmetrical with an iconic shape. Using this principle as a starting point, it only took a couple of days to design our new cone-shaped laundry bottle rather than months of expensive exploration and consumer testing.

HUDDLE UP Speed requires great communication, and the Monday all-company huddle is our way of keeping everyone moving and connected. We started the huddles in 2006, after we moved across town to a larger office that dispersed us on three floors. The huddle gives us an opportunity to re-create the environment we had back when we were in our smaller offices on Union Street; even if it only happens once a week, everyone at our headquarters is in the same room together for thirty minutes. The energy is awesome—an amalgam of meaningful discourse and locker room pep talk. Getting everyone together keeps us all aligned on everything from quarterly sales targets to what's happening on the production room floor. The value of the huddle is in reminding all that their individual contribution fits within the larger ecosystem. Speed on an organizational level requires both collective understanding and individual contribution.

ORGANIZE YOUR PEOPLE IN PODS These are cross-functional teams that sit within earshot of one another rather than in separate departments or another building. There's a laundry pod, a hand pod, even a values pod. Speed and innovation require a rapid cadence of problem solving, which requires keeping diverse minds in close contact. By combining various people with different outlooks and different skills, we foster a higher level of maturity and empathy, ensuring that everyone communicates in a cross-functional manner. Bottom line: If you want to be fast, It's essential to make sure that no one in your company is cut off from anyone else. Our pods allow an engineer and a graphic designer to work as a small team maintaining an entrepreneurial environment as the company scales.

FLAT IS FAST Racing dinghies at the age of seven, we grew familiar with the phrase "flat is fast"—because you work as hard as possible to keep your boat flat in order to move faster through the water. The same is true in corporate America, where layers of bureaucracy lead to slower decisions. The fast company is one in which everyone has the autonomy and authority to make decisions and move quickly. But that means everyone must be talented and people must be empowered to operate efficiently and independently. One way we encourage this kind of environment is by delegating a lot of authority and leadership responsibilities to our "zookeepers"—essentially, project managers on steroids. Allow us to explain: Completed work is quite literally dollars moving through the company. Rather than ask three levels of middle management to approve every decision— draining time and money in the process—zookeepers make those everyday key decisions that get us to market (and to profits) faster. A normal project manager builds a timeline and bothers people until the job gets done. Because we're organized by pod, zookeepers must bring dynamic operational insight to every discipline. They're the bridge between the conceptual work on the drawing board and the real product on store shelves. Between those two points are an infinite number of steps that touch everything from headquarters in San Francisco to factories in French Lick, Indiana, to the nameless and faceless truck drivers pulling up to loading docks in towns none of us have ever heard of.

Another way we keep the office flat is by keeping it open. Our open floor plan allows everyone to be a part of every conversation so they can stay connected and collaborative. Plus, we like being able to walk around and get a feel for what's going on. And, hey, during the stroll, maybe we post a few new ideas and progress reports up on the wiki walls so people can stay informed and quickly build upon any new ideas.

KEEP IT SIMPLE There's a reason this cliché sticks around. If things are too complicated, you'll never get things done. This is why Southwest Airlines has the best on-time arrival record—they've kept things simple by not assigning seating and using just one kind of aircraft (at least until recently). We try to keep our business simple with techniques like contracting out all of our manufacturing, allowing us to focus on core competencies like brand, sales, and product development.

▲ NO-DOOR POLICY. Silos cannot exist in a world built for speed.

Now, simple doesn't always mean easy—overthinking things is a natural result of caring so much about the business you're in—but we encourage simplicity by continually asking ourselves what we can get rid of in order to go faster. While most companies are great at adding new weekly meetings, processes, and rules (and bad at removing obsolete ones), one way we simplify things is to avoid making detailed plans and schedules longer than six months out. Inevitably, too much changes over two quarters to expect any plan to pan out.

HIRE SLOW, FIRE FAST Though we take our time hiring, we've always regretted holding on to a bad apple too long. In order to stay fast, you need to make sure you're not being slowed down by keeping the wrong people on your team. It may sound counterintuitive—why would you want to rush something as sensitive and important as firing someone? The reason is rooted in our culture. Left to fester, a bad hire can wreak havoc on a freethinking, collaborative team. Like poison, their bad energy has a way of working its way into your system, contaminating people around them. Don't waste time, energy, and focus agonizing about a bad hire. Sure, firing isn't fun, which is in part why it's always easy to come up with excuses to avoid it. Maybe you want to give the person a bit more time to fit in. Maybe you're shorthanded and you need someone in that role. But in the words of Steve Jobs, "We'd rather have a hole than an asshole."

ERROR AUTOPSY: THE BAMBOO WIPEOUT

It's obvious by now that our obsession with speed involves taking some risks and making our fair share of mistakes. But each misstep comes with copious learning opportunities, hence no obsession generates more error autopsies than kicking ass at fast.

Enter the bamboo wipe. In the interest of speed when sourcing materials, we've occasionally opted to skip the time-consuming negotiations that accompany a traditional purchasing contact, which enables you to lock in a set price for materials for a set period of time. While skipping a purchasing contract can be a gamble, the time saved can also mean the difference between beating our competitors to market—wowing consumers and making headlines—or landing on store shelves in the shadow of a larger competitor's multimillion-dollar national launch.

When the cost of materials shifts unexpectedly, however, we find ourselves at the mercy of the market. Such was the case with our initial launch of bamboo wipes. Compostable and more sustainable, bamboo is an ideal material for the disposable wipe industry—a market that produces eighty-three thousand tons of landfill waste every year in the United States. Recognizing an opportunity to be the first to bring bamboo to the category, we were excited about developing and launching as quickly as possible.

In the rush to be the first to market, we opted to not secure a long-term contract with our bamboo supplier. Soon after we launched the product (to much fanfare), the worldwide demand for bamboo skyrocketed. There was no denying it: we had overlooked the business proposition—getting the best quality at the right price going forward. Within six months, materials costs had ballooned by over 100 percent. And while the product was an instant hit with consumers, we simply could not make the margins work. Backtracking, we pulled the product, revised the formula and packaging, and ultimately relaunched the wipe with a different natural wood fiber. The upshot: We essentially had to develop the same product twice.

OUR SPEED MUSES: GENE MONTESANO AND BARRY PERLMAN, FOUNDERS OF LUCKY JEANS

For an obsession like Kick Ass at Fast, you'd expect our muse to be a company known for operating at blindingly fast speed—a Facebook, Google, or Twitter, one of those global tech giants that measures success in nanoseconds. Actually, our biggest "fast influence" comes from the founders of Lucky Jeans, who taught us that speed isn't always about being the fastest; it's about finding the right pace.

It all goes back to a conversation we had years ago with Lucky's founders, Gene Montesano and Barry Perlman, while sitting courtside at an Indiana Pacers game (appropriate, no?). Friends since childhood, Montesano and Perlman shipped the first order of Lucky Brand back in 1990. Since then, they've built their name on great-fitting, vintage-inspired jeans. Rooted in rock 'n' roll and celebrated for its unmistakable sense of humor, Lucky Brand stands for independent thinking, individual style, and a feeling as authentic as love. Recently they launched Civilianaire, a high-end line of denim and basics inspired by a vintage military aesthetic and the Japanese appreciation for minimalist jeans.

As we do with all of our entrepreneurial idols, we asked them for their best advice on winning in the fashion business. (Why not? After all, we're always look-

▲ **IT'S NOT ABOUT SPEED BUT PACE.** Gene and Barry taught us to follow the hour hand, not the minute hand.

ing for bright ideas we can appropriate to the world of soap!) We assumed that, coming from the go-go world of apparel, they would offer some insight into how they managed to keep up with ever-changing consumer tastes. And in a way, they did . . . though their advice seemed almost counterintuitive at first. "Follow the hour hand," they said, "not the minute hand."

It's a metaphor, of course. The average business follows the minute hand, getting caught up in chasing fads, spinning itself in circles until the clock runs out. But successful businesses sync their strategies to the slow-moving hour hand, maneuvering above the vagaries of turbulent business cycles.

Over time (wouldn't you know), we've come to understand that what Montesano and Perlman meant was that speed and agility have nothing to do with being the top trendsetter or the first to a fad. Kicking ass at fast is about pacing yourself—establishing a point of view that will quickly, clearly, and consistently guide you to make the best decisions, minute to minute, day to day, and year to year. It's ironic, right? Real speed is about being timeless.

obsession

5

RELATIONSHIP RETAIL

deliver retail differentiation by creating fewer but deeper relationships

RETAIL IS THE VIBRANT AND VITAL CROSSROADS where customer, vendor, marketer, and manufacturer collide. While each party's interests intersect, they rarely align perfectly—making retail one of the most brutal arenas in all of business. In such a harsh and uncertain environment, a devotion to relationship retail—Method's fifth obsession—seems almost soft, like the kind of feel-good language you'd find in corporate handbooks better left on the shelf. But in our experience, relationship retail has allowed us to become faster, better, and more competitive at what we do.

Three major trends are emerging in the retail landscape that simultaneously create challenges and great opportunities for upstart brands like Method. Consolidation—homogenization of the retail environmental as big-box retailers swallow the little guys—is shifting the balance of power toward those big retailers and creating barriers for small brands trying to penetrate the market. As we dig our way out of a protracted recession, consumers are flocking to lower-priced alternatives, further driving down pricing power and challenging branded players. And finally, as more people buy more things online (including everyday commodities), virtualization is opening direct-to-consumer sales channels and challenging the brick-and-mortar model altogether.

Not so long ago, every state had its own regional grocery chain—each of them fully stocked with regional brands and character. But even by 1996, when the two of us were just out of college, that era was ending. In the modern age of Walmart supercenters and IKEA megastores (with locations rivaling the size of many European principalities and parking lots hosting upward of fifty thousand cars a day) such quaint regional stores have essentially become museums. In their place, the megastore now pits the same brands and retailers against one another on a national scale. In the average American strip mall, consumers will invariably find some combination of Costco, Walgreen's, or Staples competing head-to-head with Kroger, CVS, or Office Depot—all chasing the same customers with the same products at the same prices.

This consolidation is producing a desperate need for differentiation. No matter where you're selling your product, you have to be able to stand out. What sets your product apart from everyone else isn't just about success anymore, it's about survival. Retailers are wising up to the fact that categories dominated by a few ubiquitous monolithic brands lock everyone into a price war. And in Walmart's shadow, few retailers can afford to keep up the fight. In response, a growing number of retailers have begun to seek their own unique product selection; the bigger the competitive arena and the greater the competitive intensity, the more retailers are calling for different choices. Rather than beat one another to death while competing to see who can offer the lowest price on the same jar of Skippy peanut butter, retailers are increasingly looking to distinguish themselves and save costs by varying their product mix.

Retailers are also fostering differentiation by introducing private, retailer-branded labels. Remember how private label (or generic goods) used to be stark black and white boxes with simple labels, like BEER or MILK? In the early days of the private label, the only thing that set it apart was that it was cheap. These products carried a negative social stigma. Most people assumed the name brand was better—and it almost always was.

Today, things have changed. Gone are the days when the private label was considered an inferior choice. The Great Recession has forced a shift in consumer thinking toward cheap chic—the idea that it's hip to be frugal—which has shattered negative consumer stereotypes of private label goods. Today's private label competes against national brands on both price and differentiation. Private labels like the beautiful O Organics line at Safeway, Kirkland Signature at Costco, and 365 at Whole Foods are all trusted, desirable choices. (Hey, we have friends who swear by Kirkland Vodka!) Retailers like IKEA, Marks & Spencer in the United Kingdom, and Trader Joe's are almost exclusively private label. The trend of hiring famous designers or partnering with other established brands is also making it difficult to distinguish private-label products from their independent counterparts. Just look at examples like Alexander McQueen for Target, Martha Stewart at Macy's, Better Homes & Gardens at Walmart, and Boots at CVS. Ironically, Kenmore and Craftsman were early pioneers in great private-label products and are now probably worth more than the Sears brand name. Today, private label accounts for approximately 20 percent of total food and beverage retail sales in the United States. Private labels have outperformed name brands in annual sales growth in nine of the last ten years.

Now, don't panic. Retail is not going to turn into a landscape of private labels that don't have any internal competitors. The popularity of private labels is cyclical, and retailers fall in and out of love with them depending on market trends. They love them for the margin gains over other value brands but quickly fall out of love when they need to mark down a product and realize there is no manufacturer to pick up the tab. Too much private label can wreak havoc on the balance sheet, so retailers strive to maintain balance. This trend does, however, put the squeeze on the middle of the market. Brands that have been built by offering just a single benefit to consumers ("streak-free glass!" or "whitening toothpaste!") are increasingly having their propositions co-opted by their customers' private labels, forcing them to spend more and more to maintain position.

At the same time, virtualization, the rise of online retailing for everyday commodities, is blurring the lines even further. How does that change the playing field? In some ways, it makes it easier for a small brand to come to market by giving it the same retail space (i.e., a Web site) as its competitors, easing some of the power big retailers have over small brands. At the same time, however, because the overwhelming majority of sales of everyday commodities is still done at brick-and-mortar retail, brands must create visibility in stores. And most people shopping online are shopping for brands and through retailers they already trust. So building presence, both online and offline, becomes the key challenge for any upstart brand.

Method is striving to become the number one home-care brand sold online. We have an advantage on the Web because the audience we cater to is Internet savvy—it's our demographic, and we have a strong social media presence. But online dominance is not about banner ads, it's about delivering a digital brand experience. Just look at Amazon, Zappos, or Soap.com, all successful online retailers that have figured out how to deliver exceptional, high-touch experiences and useful, innovative features. In contrast, bricks-and-mortar customer service continues to decline as the traditional leaders increasingly cut costs to keep pace with deep discounters. Look no further than the case study of Netflix (with its algorithm-driven recommendations, fine-tuned searchability, endless selection, and growing on-demand functionality) versus Blockbuster (which . . . well, by the time you're holding this book, Blockbuster may not even exist anymore).

The shifts of consolidation and the rise of private label are ushering in a new retail landscape characterized by hypercompetition and extreme price sensitivity, creating barriers to market entry that have all but locked small brands out of the market. Simultaneously, virtualization is challenging the very fabric of retail. As consumers grow more accustomed to the convenience and security of shopping online, new paths to market are emerging. What results is a power struggle between retailers and manufacturers—a battle between Goliaths to gain leverage, the upper hand constantly shifting back and forth. Retailers under pressure to carry ubiquitous brands bow to the power of the manufacturers that make them, accepting insolvent margins just so they don't lose that shopper who may or may not buy something else while in the store. In response, with fewer and fewer retail brands through which to sell and a low success rate on new innovations, manufacturers are forced to lower the retailers' risk by subsidizing their costs through expensive slotting fees and discounting. Key to winning in the midst of this power struggle is finding ways to help the retailer—our customer—win.

THE SHIFT FROM MANUFACTURERS TO RETAILERS

Arguably our biggest achievement over the past decade has been building distribution in mass retail channels, a process that demanded we fight for shelf space traditionally dominated by our larger and more established competitors. Believe it or not, the most expensive real estate in America today is the shelf space at your local grocery store—over $1 million per square foot—and the ecosystem currently in place is essentially designed to keep little guys like us out. Called *slotting* within the industry, the practice is arguably the biggest barrier to innovation in mass retail—big brands pay extra fees to keep their products front and center in the aisle, and the upstart brands get squeezed out. Over time, retailers grow accustomed to the added boost in their profit margins and the pay-to-play cycle continues. If this is beginning to sound a little like bribery, well, that's because it kind of is.

Not only does slotting create a cost hurdle for new brands, it also provides an incentive for retailers to discontinue the bottom 10 percent of every category after each six-month sales review, in order to resell the shelf space. And— surprise, surprise—if you've just launched a new brand, chances are you're in the bottom 10 percent. If that weren't bad enough, guess who's in charge of recommending which products get the ax? None other than the "category captain," one of the leading dominant brands! Yup, your opponent is also the referee in this game, and he's got his eye on you. The U.S. government has even considered making slotting fees illegal because of the unfair barrier they present to competition. It's worth noting that many of the strongest retailers out there (Target, Walmart, and Costco, to name a few) don't use slotting fees. For now, however, the system stands in plenty of other places.

"YOU HAVE TO CARRY TIDE"

While retailers have the power of the real estate they own, the sheer size and ubiquity of leading consumer brands means that manufacturers hold some power in this battle of Goliaths, too. Look at laundry detergent. Laundry detergent has nearly 100 percent household penetration. (The fact that it's not exactly 100 percent makes us wonder who's not doing laundry.) Tide has nearly 50 percent market share, which means that for half of the households in America, when people run out of laundry detergent, they go to the store looking for Tide. Retailers also know that no one takes the time to get in the car and drive to the store to buy only one jug of laundry detergent—you're going to stock up on the other things you need while you're there. So retailers resort to carrying Tide at wafer thin margins and advertising that they have the lowest price around, to get you into the store in the hope that you will buy other, more profitable items while you're there. Retailers don't like selling Tide for nothing, but given the power and size of the brand, they have no choice.

Exploiting this shift in power by finding ways to bring the power back to the retailer—our customer—becomes a winning strategy for Method. If the laundry category has no profit in it, we'll bring profit. If all the products are the same, we'll bring something unique. If the laundry category isn't growing (because everyone in America already does laundry) then we'll even find a way to grow the category. By holding our competitors' approaches against them, by being different and playing a different role with our customers, we become a key ally in creating our customers' success.

Obviously, there are plenty of downsides to the way things have shifted in retail in recent years. Try to compete on volume and price and you'll get sucked into a race to the bottom, crushed between big brands with more leverage and private labels with better margins. So how did we overcome these odds and extend distribution to tens of thousands of retail locations from our start in a dirty little apartment in San Francisco? Ironically, some of the same daunting retail trends that appear to make things more difficult for new brands actually present significant opportunities—and we've been able to identify a number of them simply by focusing on the key partnerships and relationships that make up our supply and distribution chain.

IF YOU'RE NOT DIFFERENT, YOU'RE DEAD

If you don't show up with a meaningful trade story, don't show up! A trade story is your proposition. It is why a retailer should take you instead of someone else. Ours is built around the three things that retailers are most starved for in the cleaning aisle: something unique, something that brings growth, and something that makes them money. As in any great relationship, it's up to you to bring something meaningful to the picture. And if you want the relationship to last, you want that something to be truly different—not just cheaper than the other guys out there. This is no easy task for a company like ours; we're always looking for something our seven ginormous competitors have missed. Our trade story is grounded in three benefits that can be applied to any category, whether you are selling soda or plasma TVs. We deliver differentiation, incremental growth, and profitability.

DIFFERENTIATION Retailers love saying, "Find it exclusively here!" If you are providing something truly different that no one else has, a retailer will hold

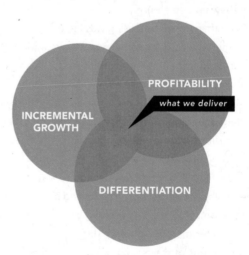

▲ **ALIGN INTEREST.** Create a trade story that aligns your interests with those of retailers. For us it's driving profitability, differentiation, and incremental growth.

you to a different standard than your competitors. Moreover, they don't have to compete on the lowest price with your product because they're the only place that carries it. You can offer differentiation over the short term by giving a retailer a one-year head start on a new item or over the long term by committing not to sell your brand to their main competition, which reduces expensive marketing support. In addition, a retailer is more likely to promote you and provide co-marketing support because of the image differentiation your brand is providing.

This strategy recently helped us launch in France with minimal resources. Representatives of other companies often ask to visit us and learn from our approach, and through one of these requests, France's second-largest retailer, Auchan, brought its entire senior leadership team to our office. They were coming in for a consulting lesson, which gave us the opportunity to sell through a consulting approach (more on this later in the chapter). After hearing about our best practices, they suggested we do business together, and we offered them a two-year exclusive in France. In return for differentiation, they were excited to support the brand, giving us generous shelf space and plenty of marketing support. The result was that we launched in a new country with few resources and ensured foundational success that we can build on.

INCREMENTAL GROWTH Retailers are craving incremental growth, so being able to demonstrate how you will help them achieve this goal is about as essential as getting your name right on your résumé. There are a lot of ways to show how you will generate incremental growth, but three are truly important when you're partnering with a retailer. Because we're talking theoretically here, we'll use buggy whips, a favorite example of our high-school economics teacher from Grosse Pointe North.

I will bring new consumers into the category because this buggy whip will inspire more people to get a buggy whip.

I will promote a new use for buggy whips that will inspire current buggy whip owners to buy a second buggy whip to have as a spare.

I will create a new category by introducing an entirely new type of buggy whip that will inspire current buggy whip owners to buy a second kind of buggy whip.

For us, incremental growth translates into a trade story that goes something like this: Our soap is so cool that it inspires people not only to clean with our product but to leave it on their countertops, where it gets seen and used more, instead of hiding it under the sink. We have actually transformed a need into a want by making cleaning products an impulse buy. This is what saved us during the Target test when we missed our sales goals. The buyer looked past gross sales and realized that we were almost 100 percent incremental to the existing category and therefore grew their overall business. That, my friend, is retail gold. The second pillar of our incremental growth story is that while our total sales might not be as big as the leading brands', sales of Method are far more likely to be incremental ones—gravy for the retailer's top (and bottom) line.

PROFITABILITY In addition to their needs for differentiation and growth, retailers' calls for profitability are becoming increasingly loud. Many retailers work on razor-thin margins and rely on mass-market, money-losing products to drive traffic to their stores. Thus many have become overly dependent on slotting fees. So if you can help a retailer drive profit, there is a good chance you will become that retailer's best friend. The way to think about this is in the simple segmentation of good, better, best. Every mature retailer strives to offer:

Good. Products at the opening price point (OPP) that deliver value (Milwaukee's Best).

Better. Usually the *big* brand lives here, as it serves the big middle of the market (Budweiser).

Best. The premium choice of the category (Sierra Nevada).

Companies make most of their profits at opposite ends of the market with either the value brands or the premium ones. This trend, well documented by Michael J. Silverstein and Neil Fiske in *Trading Up*, is leading to death in the middle for brands that don't compete in either the value or premium segments. This is happening for a couple of reasons. First, with the demise of mass media comes the demise of the mass market. Look at any category and you will see that the big mass brands that occupy the middle space are in decline or stagnant. Growth is occurring at the value end, where consumers trade down because within the category they view the choices as essentially the same, and at the premium end, where they trade up because they believe the higher quality is worth a price premium. The problem with competing in the value segment is that retailers are taking it over with private label to boost their own profit. This leaves Best as the segment where you need to be to increase profit for a retailer.

Retailers get caught up in moving volume, so you have to constantly remind their buyers that, while you may have a smaller percentage of revenue (say, even just 1 percent), you nevertheless might generate 5 percent of their overall category profits. Big guys win on scale games, but if retailers want to remain profitable, they'll need to avoid commoditization and grow your brand in their stores.

SELLING IS A TRANSFER OF EMOTION

It is a simple point, but when fulfilling your mission depends on getting people to know you and use your products, selling becomes a point of personal passion. No longer is it a pitch—a sales guy or gal trying to dupe a buyer into a big contract. It's a discussion, a collaboration, about how two companies can come together and use their common assets to create some good in the world. And do good business in the process.

While a good trade story is important, never forget that selling is, at its heart, a transfer of emotion. If this wasn't the case, you would never go on a sales call, you would just send a deck and wait for a response. But because passion is contagious, we leverage this as a big difference between us and Big Soap. Luck-

▲ **YES, EVEN WEIRD CAN HELP YOU SELL.** Next time ditch that blue-blazer steak-house sales dinner for something imaginative. If you don't get the sale, at least you will have had fun.

ily this is easy for us because we have a clear purpose and a developed culture. And if you are not passionate about what you do (particularly if you're in sales), find another job. By demonstrating passion, we can align our interests with the interests of the retailers. Once we establish that we're on the same page, it's just a question of developing our shared strategy. From there, weirdness takes all shapes and sizes. We've been known to hold sales meetings over broom ball games, show up at retailers wearing their vendor vests, and greet visiting buyers with surprise all-company pep rallies, and our sales meetings have included dinners in bed at supper clubs, *Iron Chef*–style competitions, and tequila classes. While we've yet to conduct a sales meeting entirely in song, we're close to cracking that one too.

YOU CAN'T BE FRIENDS WITH EVERYBODY

Instead of selling one bathroom cleaner to everyone in America, we want to sell everything needed to clean a home to the segment of America that is progressive environmentally, socially, and aesthetically. As we said before, we're after wallet share, not market share. That requires us to prioritize some potential customers over others, to work more deeply with those who match our demographic and psychographic target more closely.

One of the first mistakes most entrepreneurs make is overextending their brand. Method was no exception. Within just a few years of the launch of the company, Method products were all over the retail landscape. Despite our original belief in working with fewer relationships on a deeper level, we still found ourselves saying yes to the wrong retailers. We realized how hard it was to be disciplined with revenue staring us in the face. Ultimately, we had to (re)learn that some retailers just weren't the right fit for our brand.

One way to avoid stretching your brand too far is to adjust your sales goals from quantity to quality. Instead of trying to form the *most* relationships, aim to form the *best* relationships, aligning your brand with partners that have similar values and goals. You don't want to be in every store in America. If you are, the only difference is price.

Remember that growth comes with compromises. Once you've begun establishing the right relationships, reassess your goals. How big do you want to be? How far do you want to reach? We don't have an aspiration to be a $10 billion company. We have an aspiration to be a very *special* company. If focusing on the latter leads to the former, all the better.

BREAKING IN

Busting into an established category can be daunting. Here are a few strategies we've found useful.

1. **Open a test market.** Find ten local stores in your area where the manager can decide whether to carry your product. If you show up enough times, they might just say yes, and you're on your way to proving sales (which you can then take to a bigger chain).
2. **Find an alternative way in.** Even if it's not the buyer, get someone there excited. We leveraged a marketing relationship to get Target's own marketing department to help us convince their buyers.
3. **Help retailers see what's in it for them.** If it's not a big and simple story, expect radio silence. Retailers are inundated with new product ideas and pitches, so if yours doesn't have a clearly articulated *benefit for the retailer,* don't bother.
4. **Skip the trade shows.** We've done the entire circuit. Unless you're paying for direct access to buyers (at shows like Efficient Collaborative Retail Marketing), there are probably better uses for your precious capital.
5. **Offer a six-to-twelve-month exclusive.** Major retailers will value the head start on their competitors, and you'll get the opportunity to test and learn before approaching other retailers.

While it may seem as though the big brands have all the advantages when it comes to retail, Method is a case study in how smaller companies can leverage unique brand traits to build strong, long-term relationships with their retail partners. The big guys have power, resources, size, reach, and pure muscle. But relationship retail as a smaller company in the green revolution takes more strategy, risk, and entrepreneurialism.

In the spirit of seeking wallet share over market share, we decided to focus on the most valuable retailers instead of everybody. By working closely with a Target or a Kroger, we may have had a lot of eggs in one basket, but it was a sturdy basket. When you are an early-stage company, you also have to face the reality that you lack the resources to serve a lot of customers well. We could have given mediocre service and attention to a lot of retailers, but we believed we'd get a better return on our investment by allocating our resources to a few rather than spreading them thin. This gave us a strategic advantage over our Goliath competitors because it forced us to leverage our limited resources more wisely. Managing this tension takes us to our next lesson—stop selling and start consulting.

STOP SELLING AND START CONSULTING

When we started Method, we had no sales experience, so we had to rely on the skills we did have. As Eric and Alastair both came from consulting backgrounds, we relied on their client relationship skills. Instead of trying to simply sell to our retailers, we acted like consultants, treating them like clients we were trying to help. For example, before we started talking about Method, we would try to provide insight into how they could grow their business. What was their biggest growth challenge in the category—and was there anything we could do to help? We recognize that you're underserving the premium customer segment here—have you thought about trying X, Y, or Z?

Offering to help started the conversation at a place of trust and collaboration, because the retailer knew we were not concerned with selling just our own products. Of course, consultants are also some of the world's best schmoozers—and understanding when to drop the sales pitch and spend some time getting to know the buyer is an important skill.

Selling consultatively requires a few unnatural skills for a typical salesperson. First, you *do* have to take no for an answer. To be truly consultative, you must be truly objective. So if the strategy means that your product isn't right for the retailer, you have to accept that and live to fight another day, or else you will permanently tarnish your credibility as a resource. You have to be able to put yourself in the retailer's shoes, understand his or her challenges and constraints, and help navigate a path to success. This requires uncommon levels of empathy on top of objectivity. Second, you have to listen—truly listen. Salespeople are usually known for their talking; ours our known for their listening. Retailers are an enormous untapped resource of information on the market, consumers, and your competitors. Take the time to listen, and who knows what you'll learn.

It's also helpful to bring the retailer along with you—to take them behind the scenes of your business so they understand exactly what your brand is all about. Back when we were developing our first concentrated laundry detergent, we took our laundry buyer from a major retailer to New York to a design kickoff meeting at Kate Spade, who we hired as a collaborator. At about five in the morning, during last call, the buyer looked at us and said, "You are either the best salespeople I have ever met or the worst. I just can't tell." Ultimately, this retailer gave us an unprecedented four feet of space in the laundry aisle for a new product launch.

We had similar experience that same evening. Dining at Asia de Cuba, we decided to randomly ask several women seated at the same table what they thought of a couple different bottle shapes for the detergent. They eagerly gave their point of view, which was actually very insightful, and when we asked what they did for a living, we discovered they were strippers. It just goes to show that you never know where good insight will come from, and in the end we felt good launching a new laundry line that was stripper approved. What else would you expect from People Against Dirty?

To make sure this approach continues as the company grows, we hire many of our salespeople from nonsales backgrounds. We have team members who are former retail buyers, Industrial Research Institute consultants, and marketing professionals. We also help promote a retail-centric culture by doing things like having one of our retailers address the entire company when they come to visit or by closing the office once a year and sending everyone on field trips to area stores.

The abnormally strong relationships we forged with our retail partners in our start-up days have translated into profound competitive advantages. To foster stronger relationships, we invite our retail partners to participate in the product development cycle, getting their input on everything from fragrances to package design as early as the concept and ideation stage. The benefits are mutual: Retailers learn more about our target customers and how to market to them, while we gain invaluable partners on the front lines. Collaborating with retailers also guarantees that they'll have a greater stake in the eventual success of our product. Great buyers are great merchants, and we try to bring out the true merchant in the buyers we work with. Below are some of our insights into the minds of retailers.

RETAILERS ARE YOUR EYES ON THE GROUND Nobody knows consumer habits and market trends better than retailers. Sure, you could hire a consulting firm or a "cool hunter" to drum up an expensive market forecast. You could also devote precious in-house resources to market research. But why not cut to the chase? Face-to-face with shoppers every day, retailers can act as your eyes on the ground, sharing valuable, up-to-the-minute information on what, how much, and why consumers are buying certain things. In turn, retailers can learn from you. They may know more about the mainstream consumers you *want*, but you know more about the advocate consumers you *have*—from what kind of marketing they like to what they're saying about in-store displays.

RETAILERS HAVE BEEN AROUND THE BLOCK Convinced the latest innovation to emerge from your R&D lab will wow customers? Eager to shake up the category with your marketing department's ingenious new pricing strategy? Chances are, not only have others been down that road, but they probably stumbled along the way. Our retail partners regularly provide insights into prior missteps in our industry. Whether it's packaging, labeling, or weekly coupon mailers, no one knows more about what *doesn't work* on the shelves than the retailers who stock them.

RETAILERS LOVE HAVING SKIN IN THE GAME When retailers take part in the development process—helping select colors or fragrances, for example, or collaborating on a product exclusive—they're more inclined to help the product succeed. Bringing them under the tent often persuades them to provide additional support—offering an end cap or some local advertising space. For better or worse, it's their baby, too. Say a new product fails to attract consumers. A strong relationship with the retailer can mean the difference between a markdown and a write-off. When initial sales of Bloq, our ill-fated body-care line, failed to meet expectations, Target could have shipped the product right off to a discount warehouse like Big Lots. But Target had participated in the design process, had reviewed packaging concepts and helped us land on the final one, and so felt personally invested in the product's success. Rather than give up early, the retailer pulled out all the stops to help it move, putting it on end caps, keeping it on shelves months longer than they were obligated to, and collaborating with us on markdowns.

RETAILERS HAVE A FEW IDEAS OF THEIR OWN If our retail partners had their way, they'd slap our brand on everything from sneakers to cereal. That's how much they believe in our style-and-substance appeal. They also appreciate our willingness to take risks. While kicks and cornflakes may not be right for Method, retailers have pushed us to expand into new frontiers that were integral to our success. Method Baby, for example, was conceived in part with Babies R Us.

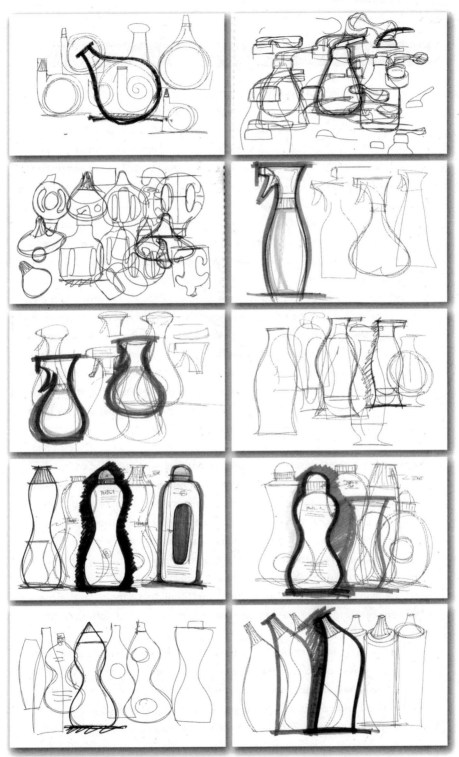

▲ **SKETCH SESSION.** We share product ideas with retailers at the earliest stages and allow them to be true merchants.

COLLABORATION AT THE SPEED OF RETAIL

Involving retailers in your development process accelerates it by giving you feedback along the way. Using prototypes and an iterative process with retailers makes decisions happen faster, because your hunches are validated quickly and definitively. It also gives your customers ownership of what you mutually create, which allows you to transcend the quick-in, quick-out cycle of listing and discontinuing typical in the grocery trade, buying critical time to build the brand in the face of big brands with big budgets.

As you see, all of our obsessions are at work in our approach to retail—and speed is a critical ingredient. A small company has to take advantage of speed and agility in its approach to retail when battling oversize competitors. By treating retailers as true partners, we include them up front at the concept stage. In our early days, we joked that we would secure a million-dollar order with one product concept sketch, but to improve your chances of success, it's important to leverage the retail perspective early. We get goosebumps when we hear a buyer say "we" when a product launches because they feel a sense of ownership. That's when you know it's a true partnership. Buyers are looking to make their mark, and we help them do this by partnering in a manner that gives them some control. Sometimes we feel like buyers when they push ideas to us or ask us to create a specific product and we are the ones saying no.

The other key advantage to this approach is that it allows you to get verbal commitment on a new product launch before investing up-front capital. In the early stages of a business, when cash is king, this brings a high level of predictability to a launch. Our process was to get one or two big retailers to look at a concept and give a verbal agreement to carry during at a specific launch window. Though it was only a verbal agreement and didn't legally bind them to anything, if the partnership was strong, we felt comfortable banking on it. With this promise in hand, we would invest capital in "cutting steel" (building a mold), and in many cases, our opening order would cover the development cost, letting us break even at launch.

But this all depends on the ability to execute fast. The model does not work if you get a verbal promise and can't deliver it until eighteen months later; by then the buyer has probably been promoted and left the job, or consumer tastes have changed and your product is no longer on trend. However, you also can't ask your people to work 24/7 during the weeks leading up to every product

BUILD ON PROOF

We like to use a "graduation strategy" to work our way up with retailers and build confidence in the relationship. We might ask a skeptical retailer to try some hand soap first and see how things go. Once consumers take note and sales pick up, maybe they'll want to introduce more products. When Duane Reade tested our hand soap next to brands like Softsoap and Dial, our sales soared. The retailer began bringing in more and more products, graduating to a special twenty-item display. As sales grew, so did our footprint in the store. Today, if you walk into a Duane Reade in New York City, you'll find more than fifty Method items.

---

launch. We've found that the way to balance the need for speed and the need for happy employees is by not launching with all retailers at once. With a broad launch, you set the stakes high, elevating the risk and putting your team in a high-pressure position where they're more inclined to think conservatively. It's the difference between opening a play on Broadway or testing it in a small theater around the corner. In the spirit of test and learn, we like to start at a few retailers quickly and expand to more over time only if a product sells well, ensuring a strong foundation. Take Smarty Dish, our dishwasher detergent. We started by placing the product in a few select locations to test the waters. After gauging consumer response and making a few tweaks, we were confident it was resonating and ready for prime time. Remember that it can be just as expensive to pull a product from the market as it is to launch it, due to markdowns (what a retailer charges you for putting it on clearance), so you should make sure it works before overinvesting in distribution. This is one way we leverage the beta test from our obsession to kick ass at fast (see page 146).

ERROR AUTOPSY: GETTING NAKED FOR WHOLE FOODS

Even though we share a purpose and a similar branding strategy, Method and Whole Foods haven't always seen eye-to-eye. As a matter of fact, it took years of negotiations and an entirely new product line before we got in the door.

From the beginning, Whole Foods objected to our use of dyes. Whole Foods tests products rigorously, and even though we showed them our dyes were safe and degradable, it was a nonstarter for them. Unfazed, we made multiple visits to Whole Foods headquarters in Austin, negotiating, struggling, and attempting to quell their skepticism. We argued on behalf of our dyes, showing scientifically their environmental benefits, and we pointed to Method's cutting-edge design, comparing the brand's bright, fun lifestyle appeal to the dusty, boring products in Whole Food's "green" aisle. But even after a local Whole Foods in Cupertino started stocking Method with great success, the corporate headquarters still wouldn't budge. We took it personally.

One thing we have learned is that there's no such thing as winning an argument with a retailer. Prove a buyer wrong and you're liable to burn a bridge. It didn't matter that we could prove with life-cycle analyses that putting a non-toxic, degradable dye in the product was far greener than putting a color (even

▲ THE POWER OF RELATIONSHIP RETAIL.
Our m-spot brand blocking statements disrupt
the cleaning aisle.

white!) in the plastic bottle. Whole Foods had a unilateral policy against colorants, and it was a matter of philosophy. They were not impressed with our arguments, and to their credit, they stuck to their principles. Whole Foods 1, Method 0.

But driven to make the relationship work, we returned to the lab and began working with Method's green chefs on an entirely new line of products. If Whole Foods didn't like dyes, there would be no dyes. We had a small but vocal group of advocates who loved our brand but were "no fragrance" people. We put the two nays together and, returning to Austin, unveiled Method's newest invention: Go Naked, a line of several products that were completely dye- and fragrance-free. We presented them along with some of our tried-and-true items that also happened to be dye-free. Whole Foods said they'd consider it.

Weeks later, we sat in front of the phone in a tiny conference room. Whole Foods said, "We have some great news for you guys! You're in—nationally—with twenty-three items." We opened the door and shouted, *"We are in Whole Foods!"* The office erupted in cheers. Since then, it's been a strategic, highly collaborative, supportive relationship that has produced significant mutual benefit to the bottom lines of both companies.

Today, Whole Foods stocks some forty Method products. By finding common ground that respects the right each party has to its own philosophy, yet defines common areas in which to build business together, we have created a partnership as deep and meaningful as any we have. And despite the fact that the chain is much smaller than our other retailers (Whole Foods has only about 300 stores compared to 1,600 for Target and 1,700 for Lowe's), Whole Foods is one of our top customers in sales volume.

OUR RETAIL MUSE: TARGET, A PARTNERING PIONEER

Target has been a true muse to us in its ability to bring class to mass. The Target people understand how to invest in something and then sell it. They are skilled at recognizing, collecting, and presenting the early evidence of a mass trend before any other major retailer. In essence, great merchants like Target are curators. Our original business plan was full of inspiration from the way Target was reinventing the idea of design at mass. We leveraged Michael Graves's toilet-bowl brush as evidence of America's growing desire for everyday design and Target's groundbreaking collaboration with designers like Isaac Mizrahi as proof that retailers were rethinking branded relationships. It seems commonplace now to see famous designers collaborating with mass retailers, but a few years ago, this was revolutionary ground broken by Target.*

In our original pitch to Target, we coined the idea of "designer commodities" by showing them a Karim Rashid–designed dish soap bottle. While we typically give Target a hard time about our first rocky meeting and being told we had a "snowball's chance in hell" of being picked up, it's remarkable that America's third-largest retailer would give a company like us a shot with full end caps in 10 percent of their chain, followed by a national rollout months later.

So what have we stolen from Target? Well, besides a few visitor badges that we forgot to return, we have stolen the meaning of being a great merchant—investing in something and then selling it, rather than purely buying. Too many retailers are run by "buyers," and the art of being a great merchant continues to disappear in mass retailing. Merchants have intuition and instinct. They understand that they have the power to create a trend and influence their customers instead of following the prevailing winds. Trader Joe's is a great merchant, as are Whole Foods, Pharmaca, Lowe's, and Bed Bath & Beyond, to name a few. They have a point of view and are willing to partner with us to set a trend rather than following the existing one at a lower price.

Many people still assume we are Target's private label because it's the retailer they most closely associate us with. While our design is original, we did steal the idea that design can be democratized. They helped give us the confidence that combining high style with low prices was a winning formula, and then they gave us the support to prove it on a national stage. See you at the local!

---

* Unlike our other muses, you may have noticed that we don't name an individual at Target who inspired us. That's because we could fill a book with all the people there who have played the role of muse to our business and mission. This is also in keeping with the Target culture, which celebrates collective efforts over individuals in the spirit of great teamwork.

obsession

WIN ON PRODUCT EXPERIENCE

be product-centric and deliver remarkable product experiences

IT'S NO SECRET THAT MODERN CONSUMERS ARE overwhelmed with choice in every category. *The Paradox of Choice, The Tyranny of Choice, The Art of Choosing*—the trend is so pervasive that even choosing which book to read on the topic is an exercise in decision making. In search of the broadest possible appeal, products are researched and group-thinked into the ground, resulting in brands that we neither love nor hate and that must be advertised incessantly in order to generate even mild consumer interest. And thanks to increased global competition, widespread access to the Web, cheap labor, and the declining cost of formulating and manufacturing products, rival brands are increasingly working with the same tools, leading to cluttered stores, jammed warehouses, and endless inefficiencies. Though the trend is true in almost every consumer category, from cable television to online shopping, you need look no further than that modern-day arena of capitalism, the grocery store.

While the average supermarket has some 40,000 products, or SKUs (stock-keeping units), the average family gets an estimated 80 to 85 percent of what it needs from just 150! Typical shoppers (those who don't have a lot of free time on their hands) will ignore 39,850 items in that store. Even if shoppers were able to glance at every box, bag, and label in every aisle during their typical thirty-minute trip, they'd have less than 0.05 seconds to assess each product.

Overwhelmed by bland choices and parity prices, consumers are increasingly relying on memories and emotions to guide their purchasing decisions over rational criteria alone. Studies of the brain show that emotion acts five thousand times faster than logic, and in a culture pressed for time, seconds (even split seconds) count. So while it may not seem like a major concern to the average consumer, behind all those choices, a battle for experience is raging among brands and retailers, reshaping how businesses compete. Seeking to stand out, businesses are designing better experiences by tapping into our emotional-memory-based decision making.

For a bit of background on why, let's examine the motivations behind every purchasing decision. We like to think of this in terms of a pyramid. (Yeah, we like pyramids.) At the bottom of the motivations pyramid are *needs*—the broadest motivations at work in any consumer category. If you're shopping for a car, these might be things like enough room for your whole family or great safety features. Easy enough. Next up on the pyramid: *wants*—anything from a leather-appointed interior to a V-8 engine or a convertible top. *Desires* take the top spot, representing, quite literally, whatever your heart desires. Note that we're now in emotional territory—for example, the desire to feel good about yourself or your place in society by buying a certain brand. This might sound something like "I want to be seen as a responsible citizen (so I'll buy a Prius)" or "I want to feel successful (perhaps a Mercedes)." Over time, as a category matures and basic needs and wants become satisfied, consumers trade their way up the pyramid toward greater and greater satisfaction . . . ideally, at least. Of course, if you really want your advocates to climb the brand pyramid with you, you'll need to do some work.

STAND OUT WITH EXPERIENCE

In order to compete on desires of your customers, you can no longer rely on your product alone. A cool bottle, a nice fragrance, a whole bunch of extra-sudsy bubbles—these may be things people want, but they really don't resonate that much with our customers on an emotional level. Let's go back to the car-buying example: The desire to feel cool by buying a top-of-the-line convertible is not satisfied by just buying the car and parking it in the driveway. It's fully realized when you actually go out and drive it with the top down! Bottom line: It's not the product that fulfills the desire, it's the experience of using it.

Now, in order to really get people to desire your product, you need to create a great experience. This is harder than it seems. Think about it—how many great brand experiences do you have each week? The gas station, the grocery store, your last flight? Not exactly. Despite all the money brands spend on consumer research, there are very few customer experiences worth talking about today. Look at any mature category—tires, tissues, tape, you name it—and while

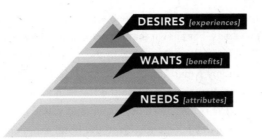

▲ **PRODUCTS FULFILL NEEDS.** Experiences
fulfill desires. The abundance of society has
oversatisfied most of our material needs so
today we have to compete on more emotional
sensibilities.

you'll find very little consumer disappointment, you'll also discover very little room for differentiation. All the needs and wants are met! But consider the unlimited opportunity to deliver a better *experience*—in every category, from products to retail to service. What's a better experience? It's one that's memorable, remarkable, or unexpected in some way. It's what keeps people coming back to you instead of your competitors. Like it or not, a quality product just isn't enough. Today, quality is only the price of entry.

It's no wonder we're craving more experiences in our lives. With most of our basic needs satisfied in our world of plenty, we are becoming a much more

Dec 10, 2010

Dear Method,
I had to write you and tell you that I was extremely motivated to clean my entire home last night... thanks to you! It takes a lot to make me want to clean... it's such a thankless job! I actually hate housekeeping but Method is just so fashionable and refreshing, how can I resist.

– Sarah

experience-driven society. Ryan Howell, a psychology professor at San Francisco State University, has shown that experiences make us happier than material goods. (Check out Howell's work with the Personality and Well-Being Lab.) In a surplus economy (where most needs and desires are met), experiences trump possessions. You can see this in the travel industry, wherein brands like Virgin Airlines and W Hotels make us feel hip and young on the road. A couple of decades ago, Holiday Inn standardized the hotel experience under the tagline, "The best surprise is no surprise." In contrast, the W Hotel promises to do just the opposite—surprise you with wonderful experiences!

ROOM TO BREATHE   We knew we didn't stand a chance if we tried to compete in our category on needs and wants alone. After all, our competition wasn't just five hundred times our size; the leaders also had a hundred-year head start on us! That's a century of identifying (and often contriving) every imaginable consumer need or want and satisfying it with 99.9 percent efficacy. There aren't a lot of people walking around wishing they could find a better dish soap. For decades, the brands that washed, cleaned, and disinfected the best won the most customers. But after more than a century of unprecedented innovation, most of our cleaning needs had been satisfied! Moreover, most of the leading brands had deep brand equity. They made their name during the golden age of mass media, capturing the broadest general consumer needs, like streak-free windows or the stain-fighting power in laundry detergent. This often resulted in mediocre or me-too products becoming bestsellers because all that marketing muscle could compensate for the lack of a unique product. Catching up and overtaking these giants would be like trying to out-Clorox Clorox: It wasn't going to happen. Outspending them was out. Since a lavish marketing budget is not a luxury most start-ups have at their disposal, there's a greater emphasis on developing a remarkable product that delivers a great experience.

Without the R&D budgets or the consumer-research departments of our rivals, we had two choices: give up—or move the goal posts, redefining the battleground around experiences, not just solutions. As the vast majority of CPG had been commoditized, we couldn't claim to be another cleaner that just, well, cleaned. Don't get us wrong, we know cleaning power is very important, and we work to make sure our products kick ass without all the nasty chemicals in them, but today a product that works is merely where the race begins. For us, we needed to do what the competition couldn't. We needed to make cleaning a better experience. We had to make it fun.

Let's face it, cleaning is still not enjoyable for most people, and there is nothing scarcer in it than pleasure. But people pay a premium for what is scarce. We've listened to women in focus groups articulating the challenge and complexity of trying to be a modern woman—every bit the homemaker her mother was but also the career person her father was—explaining how Method, *our brand*, took the drudgery out of cleaning and helped them manage this very personal challenge.

▲ **CONSUMERS PAY A PREMIUM FOR WHAT IS SCARCE.** In cleaning there is nothing more scarce than fun. Cleaning naked is sadly scarce too.

This transition from rational propositions to emotional propositions is the crux of Method's obsession with product experience. Dating back to our earliest days, this insight has had a profound influence on everything we make. With the convergence of these macrotrends and a heavy passion for product, we set out to create a company that would win on product experience. To do this, we needed to create an organization that was highly product-centric. If you look at which consumer product companies are really winning today, you'll see they're all great at product execution—Apple, Dyson, Nike, BMW, just to name a few. The world is shifting toward favoring organizations that are fluent at creating truly great products, particularly products that deliver consumer experiences as the meaningful differentiator. At Method, we are a product-centric company. Everything starts with creating a killer product, and after that, everything flows naturally.

> I wish more money and time was spent on designing an exceptional product, and less on trying to psychologically manipulate perceptions through expensive advertising.
>
> **—Phil Kotler, professor of marketing,**
> **Kellogg School of Management**

GREAT EXPERIENCES DRIVE GREAT MARKETING Not that many years ago, if you were launching a new product, you would have your PR team send a press kit to the most influential magazine, newspaper, and television editors in hopes of positive coverage. Without even trying the product, they might be positively influenced by your beautiful press kit or the engaging personality of your spokesperson. But today, thanks to social media and online retailers like Amazon that allow any user to post an opinion, everyone has become an editor. Every consumer holds the power to make or break your product with an online review or a quick Yelp that can be seen by everybody and lives forever. Remember that threat from your seventh-grade teacher about putting something in your permanent record? Today that record really exists and it's called the Internet. If you put a subpar product on the market that does not meet consumer expectations, all of your editors will burn you and one day your grandchildren will hear about it.

Consider the "Twitter effect" on movies. The first movie ever to suffer a double-digit single day drop after opening was *Bruno*, starring Sasha Baron Cohen. Why? Because millions of people walked out of the movie theater on

★★★★☆ Fantastic floor cleaner. ...

> Fantastic floor cleaner. I've tried everything because I have a dog who constantly likes to leave paw prints on the floor. I also really try to buy natural products. This floor cleaner works very well on my hardwood... it leaves it very clean and shiny and it smells fantastic. I recently ran out and had to run to the store and buy a competitive product. It had nowhere near the same gleaming, lasting effect. I threw it out and returned to Method.

▲ **TODAY EVERYONE IS AN EDITOR.** Consumers have the power to toast or roast you for the world to see.

opening night and tweeted, texted, posted, blogged, and Facebooked about what a crappy movie it was! So the next day, a lot fewer people went to see it. This was dramatically different from Cohen's previous movie, *Borat*, which was a great film (to most anyway) that aimed small and built a cult following based on word-of-mouth.

In today's transparent world, alive with social chatter, your product is your marketing. Consumers love to evangelize product experiences that are emotional. Deliver a bad product experience and consumers will roast you. Why call a customer-service number when you can go public with your disappointment? Worse, their comments and reviews will live online long after you've discontinued the dud or given them a rebate. On the flip side, if you deliver a great product experience, consumers will be eager to share their discovery with millions rather than just their close friends or neighbors. Today experiences really matter because they inspire word-of-mouth—both good and bad.

To thrive in this new environment, we think of "cutting steel" as a media expense. Cutting steel is what you do when you build a mold to create a custom product—you buy a big block of steel and then cut it into a mold in the shape you want. It's an expensive process with little room for error; it's why many companies choose generic or stock bottles instead of investing in custom ones. But when we compared the cost of cutting steel to the cost of marketing, the ROI suddenly started looking much better. For us, it costs an average of $150,000 to create a new unique bottle design, which looks expensive compared to selecting a stock bottle with no tooling cost. But if we saved that $150K and invested it in marketing instead, what would it buy us? Not much. Not even one quarter-page ad in a national magazine. Yet the unique bottle design can generate millions in free press and social media attention! Not to mention the marketing power it will retain, capturing retailers' attention, landing better shelf space, and inspiring impulse purchases from new customers. Our belief was that if we created a product that exceeded expectations, people would talk about it and drive word-of-mouth. Because Method could never win the advertising battle by shouting louder, we needed the product to shout for us. Too many companies create products with the assumption that a healthy marketing budget will ensure success. But we believe you should go into any product development process with the assumption there will be no marketing support and that the product needs to be special and differentiated enough to stand on its own. Marketing should be rocket fuel to propel a great product, not the Hail Mary for a mediocre product.

GREAT EXPERIENCES COME FROM A CLEAR POINT OF VIEW How many brainstorming sessions have you been to where someone asks, "How would Virgin do this?" or "How would Disney do this?" When you ask this question about a brand not your own, you have a problem. The starting point for great products is a crystal-clear point of view. If you lack that, everything is an uphill battle. Look at the companies that produce the greatest product experiences— Dyson, Apple, Virgin, Guinness, Mini Cooper . . . they all have a clear POV of who they are and their role in the world. Others have lost their way, trying to be everything to everyone. Take IHOP, for example. While the International House of Pancakes once had a crystal-clear vision—right down to the Bavarian-style architecture of its restaurants—today's IHOP is too focused on selling dinner instead of making unique and killer pancakes from all over the world. It's as if the executives at IHOP started asking themselves, "How would Denny's do it?"

At Method, we ask ourselves, "How would Method do it?" We make sure our brand is inspiring to us and that it serves as the starting brief for anything we work on. To us, Method's POV is inclusive, optimistic, simple, and aspirational— or, to take it directly from our brand DNA statement, "smart, sexy, and sustainable." Internally, we often hear people say they can't start working on something until they have a brief. We like to remind them that "the brand is the brief!" So how do we make our products smart, sexy, and sustainable?

To help articulate our point of view, we defined our experience pillars— standards which every Method product experience must fulfill. Many brands create *brand pillars*, but consistent with our philosophy of baking the marketing

▲ **TO US, CUTTING STEEL IS A MARKETING EXPENSE.** There is no better marketing investment than creating killer packaging.

into the product, we have replaced them with *experience pillars*. To transform mundane chores into pleasurable experiences, we think in four dimensions: design, fragrance, efficacy, and environment. Once a product meets Method's standards in each dimension, it's ready for the market. For example, the latest iteration of our dish soap has a pump that eliminates the drippy mess common to standard bottles, its fragrances are more akin to something you'd find in an expensive candle, and the formula is gentle enough to be safe on the skin yet powerful enough to stand up alongside its mainstream competitors. The ben-

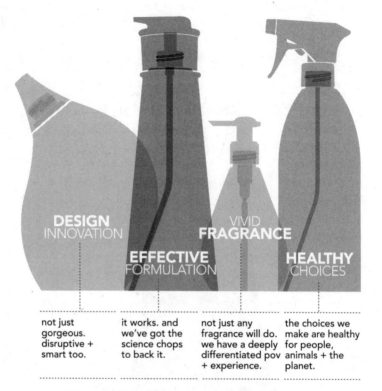

DESIGN INNOVATION	EFFECTIVE FORMULATION	VIVID FRAGRANCE	HEALTHY CHOICES
not just gorgeous. disruptive + smart too.	it works. and we've got the science chops to back it.	not just any fragrance will do. we have a deeply differentiated pov + experience.	the choices we make are healthy for people, animals + the planet.

▲ **EXPERIENCE PILLARS.** By combining style and substance, we deliver a multidimensional product experience.

efits of this experiential formula are twofold: The consumer gets a better experience, and Method gets a competitive advantage. After all, products can be copied, but experiences are one of a kind.

An important aspect of a clear point of view is that it helps you carefully edit and decide not only what to do, but also what not to do. Arguably the most important decision when creating a new product or service is how to simplify by making decisions about what it should not be or what to take out. Too many products are full of "feature creep" that unnecessarily overcomplicates them and creates a product that does everything well but nothing great. In our over-complicated world, the need for simplicity is only going to grow stronger. Apple, In-N-Out Burger, and Trader Joe's got this right. Now will someone please solve our overly complicated living-room entertainment systems so the babysitter can watch TV without a thirty-minute tutorial on which remote to use!

Perhaps the most elegant aspect of Method's POV is how it lends itself to scalability. Think about it: design a better product and what do you have? One good product. Design a better experience, however, and you've got a platform for countless products. This is, in part, why Method has been able to grow so quickly, disrupting each new category with the same strategy. Product experience is about being refreshing to consumers. It's about looking for areas where we can be distinct. In some categories, being refreshing and distinct almost looks easy—as was the case when Method turned its attention to baby care products.

As the company was growing up, we all started having babies, so when we couldn't find baby products with a strong sense of individual design and a belief in greener solutions, we decided to create them ourselves. Conscientious parents love the mild ingredients—like rice milk and mallow—and they applaud the lack of harmful chemicals, like phthalates and parabens (which major baby brands had been hiding off-label for years). But it wasn't ingredients alone that helped our baby line stand out. Keeping in line with our obsessions, the cartoony bottles were eye-catching and made from sustainable materials. And the line was designed with the real-world experiences of busy, preoccupied parents in mind. Our diaper cream features a one-handed pump for no-mess usage and our baby wash includes an oversize cap that doubles as a rinsing cup. As stand-alone fea-

▲ WE DON'T SELL PRODUCTS. WE SELL A PHILOSOPHY.

tures, each was a minor triumph in industrial design; collectively, the line exemplifies the dynamic power of Method's obsession with product experience.

GREAT EXPERIENCES ARE BOTH EMOTIONAL AND RATIONAL Most companies underestimate the power of emotional differentiation, focusing instead on functional differentiation. Rational, fact-based, "hard" attributes always play well in boardrooms and focus groups, but they don't reflect the real way consumers think and act. Consumer loyalty is the result of a brand's ability to stand out on both functional and emotional attributes. Sure, most consumers consider functional attributes more important than emotional ones, but what if all your competitors have the same functional attributes? You've got to stand out somehow—and studies have shown that brands that distinguish themselves on emotional attributes can capture 60 percent greater loyalty (source: Forrester Research).

So to achieve high levels of loyalty, today's new brands have to focus their resources on a select few functional attributes on which they can double down—often requiring them to divert resources from less important ones. An example in nearby Berkeley, California, is Berkeley Bowl grocery stores. It's a foodie's paradise, with a ridiculous selection of fresh produce and exotic goods. Problem is, it's a customer-service nightmare, with long checkout lines, overwhelmed stockers, and crowded aisles. The store purposely overinvests on delivering great selection while willingly sacrificing on service. Walking through the store, you can't help but wonder, "Don't these guys value customer service? Is the produce that good?" For a select group of devoted Berkeley residents, it is—and Berkeley Bowl has built its business on that emotional response. Most of us, however, would rather go to a place that satisfies our desire for strong quality and great service. This is the most effective way to deliver emotionally distinct experiences—by linking them to the "shared values" of your brand and a specific consumer. This reinforces the importance of mission, purpose, and point of view. That's why, at Method, we match the sensory experience to our advocates' shared value for "the love of clean."

Let's start with the toilet. Toilet-bowl cleaner is a great example of the importance of ensuring that every experience has a strong functional side. This was one of the first products we wanted to do back in 2001, but Method didn't enter the category until 2008. The tale of how Lil' Bowl Blu made it to market after seven years of trial and error is a testament to our unflagging devotion to winning on product experience.

Purifiers of porcelain, sanitizers of stool—toilet-bowl cleaners (TBCs) were on Method's hit list from the very beginning. Sure, they aren't glamorous, but they represent everything we wanted to change about the industry. First off, they are ugly—the black sheep of the home-care family. Everyone has them but would rather forget about them. Worse, they are among the most toxic products in the home, literally covered in warnings and instructions for contacting the nearest poison control center if you accidentally ingest even the tiniest amount. Most odious of all, they suck to use. Consumers either have to lift off the heavy lid to get into the grimy tank every few weeks or get down on their knees and scrub away, their face just inches from the smelly bowl.

Ugly, toxic, unpleasant to use—toilet cleaners were right in Method's sweet spot. Soon after setting up our first lab, we began experimenting with nontoxic cleaning agents for the toilet. Problem was, toilet cleaners were toxic for a reason; phosphates and strong acids were the only things strong enough to wipe out the formidable brew of mineral deposits, rust, and bacteria that toilet bowls are famous for. There were organic cleaners on the market, but they were nowhere near as effective—and the toilet bowl was the last place people wanted

▲ COMPROMISES DON'T SELL IN
A CROWDED MARKET.

to cut corners on effectiveness. Even the most environmentally conscious home owner was generally willing to overlook the skull and crossbones on the back of the bottle if the front of the bottle promised to kill *every last germ*.

Our team of green chefs tried liquids, creams, and gels. They sent prototypes home with employees, complete with powders, scrubbers, and sponges. Nothing worked. There was constant temptation to do something substandard because we just couldn't make organic acids work as well as inorganic, toxic crap. But we didn't.

Years passed as we chased the formula like a white whale. No matter how desperate the company was for revenues, no matter how much advocates wailed about how the company was "missing a huge opportunity" (and a toilet cleaner was by far the most requested new product), Method still refused to put out a product that didn't work as well or better than its mainstream, toxic rivals. Then in early 2008, one of our engineers cracked the code that had stymied every Method green chef. Employing lactic acid in combination with some novel renewable surfactants, he finessed a liquid formula strong enough to clean as well as the big brands (without any scrubbing) and safe enough that consumers could rub it on their hands without poisoning themselves. Having waited the better part of a decade for a technology that satisfied the brand's uncompromising obsession with product experience, Method didn't wait a minute more. Debuting in a bladder-shaped bottle and eucalyptus mint scent, Lil' Bowl Blu went straight to national distribution.

Delivering on emotional experiences means engaging the senses, for the senses are the fast track to human emotion. But how many brands actually make full use of them? When people talk about "clean," they usually describe it as the "feeling of clean." Yet there was nothing that felt clean about most cleaners. The sensory experience of using cleaners requires you to hold your breath when using them, leave the room afterward, and then hide the package under the counter because it's so ugly. Somewhere in the history of clean, consumers had been made to believe that if it doesn't make you cry, it must not be working. What's clean about that? We created a new sensory experience with a clean design that appeals to our aesthetic sense, formulas that let us actually feel clean, and fragrances that make a room smell beautiful—not like bleach. We also worked to add touch experiences with packaging that is organic in shape and made from materials that invite touch. The result is a superior sensory experience that elevates the mundane task of cleaning. All great brands have rational, emotional, and sensory values, so we work hard to ensure that Method delivers on all three.

GREAT EXPERIENCES CAN BE SOFT To generate growth, companies seem to love "hard" product innovation—the type of expensive breakthroughs that require engineers and PhDs to toil away deep in the lab. Think Teflon, Viagra, or the Segway scooter. The challenge with this type of innovation is that it's expensive and high risk because it requires a lot of marketing dollars to educate consumers, not to mention the cost of developing the product itself. And because mass advertising is not as effective as it once was, it's becoming more lengthy and expensive to recapture this type of significant R&D investment. The growing glut of technology and patents is creating a lot of noise, making it harder to predictably execute big innovations. What if your amazing new product doesn't take off?

On the flip side, soft innovators establish new standards for quality, experience, and sales in their categories without actually doing anything profoundly innovative.

At Method, we try to balance soft and hard innovations. Don't get us wrong, we love big innovation—like our radical 8x laundry detergent, which has received global accolades—but many companies underestimate the power of soft innovation, which can enhance the consumer experience and drive massive differentiation within a category. The advantage of a soft innovation is that it treads lightly on the R&D budget, requires less marketing support because consumers "get it" right away, and is predictably successful because the idea is familiar and the consumer learning curve is quicker.

Despite this comparably minimal risk, soft innovations have the power to disrupt or shift entire categories. Consider our cucumber all-purpose cleaner, our teardrop hand wash, or our new pump dish soap. Similar products have been done before, but each of ours brings a new scent, shape, or interaction to the customer experience.

For us, soft innovation includes the fragrance, design, and witty personality of our products. None of this is individually groundbreaking, but collectively it has a big impact. Going back to the original idea of "Aveda for the home," bringing a personal-care approach to home care was revolutionary, but the steps to get there were very evolutionary.

We build emotional points of difference into every product to create an engaging consumer experience. We do this by dramatically challenging existing alternatives on every front, from the use of unexpected fragrances like sea minerals to packaging copy that talks about angry squirrels. Great experiences are about being human, and humans want to be surprised. Basic categories like soap

powerful, non-toxic cleaning is not a myth. we're still working on the unicorns.

we help you put the hurt on dirt

grease + grime don't stand a chance. not with powergreen™ technology in your grasp. each squirt, in all its lovely non-toxic glory, delivers a powerful cleaning punch with naturally derived, biodegradable ingredients. cleaners made from corn + coconut break down dirt, leaving nothing behind but the pleasant scent of victory.

c t s w g
counters tile stone wood glass

▲ EXPERIENCE IN THE DETAILS. Unexpected gestures help your product bond with consumers.

offer few opportunities for differentiation, so you have to sweat the details. The way the label feels in your hand, the shape of the bottle on your counter, the sound of the trigger being squeezed, the writing on the back of a bottle that makes you chuckle, even the little surprise of an owner's manual inside a candle box. Soft innovations collectively create an experience whenever you provide something different and unexpected.

Appropriation is a great technique for creating soft innovations. It's the act of taking a small part from something created by someone else and repurposing it for new or unexpected use. It's a fancy word for stealing (on a small scale), but it's vital to any artistic business. We "steal" all the time. We stole the idea for the huddle from Innocent, and we stole the fragrance idea of sea minerals from Bare Essentials. Take the upside-down dish soap, inspired by a stapler that sits on its end for easier use, or our original squeeze-and-pour laundry detergent bottle design, borrowed from ACT mouth rinse. We invite you to steal ideas from us. These are victimless crimes. Because there's a big difference between appropriating an idea from a foreign category and doing a knock-off.

Creating a knock-off (stealing other people's work to compete directly

▲ **ONE + ONE = NEW.** Our inspiration wall with souvenirs from trend trips around the world.

against them) says you're not only an asshole, but you also lack the talent to come up with your own original ideas. (Can you tell we deal with this all the time?) But appropriating ideas from another category is about being inspired and translating someone else's innovation to a new purpose. It's about spotting a trend in a distant category or country and recognizing that the same consumer motivation being satisfied there could also be satisfied in your category. It's a way to create more predictable innovation, because you are taking something proven and applying it to your product. In essence, the brand concept for Method—bring personal care to home care—was an appropriation play. We looked for ways to translate what people loved about personal care and brought it to home care. Beautiful fragrances, like lavender, bottle designs that made a personal statement, and formulas that were healthy to touch—all stolen from our friends a few aisles away.

We have specific categories that we continually look to for inspiration. Ours include housewares, cosmetics, and functional beverages, but we don't limit it just to these categories. The idea for our biodiesel shipping program that allows us to ship products using veggie oil was borrowed from local food distributors in San Francisco. We challenge you to use appropriation to avoid the gravitational pull of your category and apply lessons from others that will help achieve the vision you have set for yourself.

Whether you are inspired by an unrelated category or putting a unique spin on a small detail of your packaging, soft innovation will help you build great experiences without reinventing the wheel with every product you make.

GREAT EXPERIENCES ARE POLARIZING Experiences are inherently personal, so don't expect everyone to love everything you do. In fact, attempting to please everyone is the surest way to design a boring product. In our increasingly fragmented consumer world, it is better to upset 90 percent of the people while capturing the attention and interest of the other 10 percent than it is to be merely OK to all of them. In other words, it is better to be something to somebody than nothing to everyone. Consider the example of Cadillac. Once the icon of automotive design excellence, through the 1980s and '90s Cadillac languished. It had gone from being a vibrant and coveted brand, symbol of edgy success, to being the choice of the Geritol crowd. Badly in need of reinvention, instead of sticking with the trend at the time of rounded, bubblelike styling, Cadillac stepped out with a hard-edged, angular look that was a departure not only from its heritage, but from the automotive design orthodoxy of the time. Many hated it. But those who liked it *loved* it. By embracing the power of polarization and doing something daring and unexpected, GM created a product experience unlike any other and reinvigorated the once tired Cadillac brand.

Consumer research is designed to find the solution with the broadest appeal, yet the most successful products always start with a small following. There will always be a gravitational pull to create a product with broad mass appeal by sanding off the edges on what makes it unique or differentiated. But compromises don't sell in a crowded market, and you can't let the remarkability of your product be squeezed out before anyone has a chance to see it. Method experiences this tension all the time with consumers who believe you need to have nuclear-strength chemicals to get something clean and others who believe that if a product contains harsh chemicals, it can't possibly be considered clean. Guess which worldview we serve? If you want someone to love your product experience and generate passion, someone else will probably hate it.

GREAT EXPERIENCES COME FROM GREAT TEAMS Over the past few decades, many companies have driven growth by incremental improvement in efficiencies of manufacture and quality of product. As a result, many Fortune 500 companies have filled their ranks with employees who excel at execution rather than innovation. Most companies don't have the type of people who are hardwired to come up with disruptive innovation, and if they have them, chances are they're not in the right position to effect change.

Here's the reality about a great product development process: It's not much of a process. There is no magical system you can put in place that leads to consistent innovation. Innovation is about blazing new trails and discovering something entirely new. The role of process is to be sure you land in a predictable place each time. Process is your friend when it comes to hitting timelines, cost goals, and critical business parameters, but can be your enemy in that mystical place where creative concepting and idea generation occur.

When we're working toward an innovation, we try to keep the process as messy as possible, but with a few critical steps interspersed. In other words, we get rid of process wherever we can, and use it only when necessary. Designers, creatives, engineers, and formulators are encouraged to begin work before the brief is set, before the product specs are started, and we make sure people know the product ideas well in advance. Since the brand is the brief, everyone is working from the same idea—how do we make our products smart, sexy, and sustainable? With our wiki walls in place, ideas can start flowing and being shared, and because we prototype everything at every stage to make the conversation tangible, ideas are easy to understand and build upon.

Once we start to home in on a strategic direction, we use two stage gates to drive the work and provide outside perspective. The first is with advocates, and the second is with retailers. With advocates we perform consumer auditions, essentially tryouts for a new product, in which we get honest feedback by putting a fully articulated product in people's hands. Then we take the feedback from these auditions, tweak and optimize, and then share the results with our retailers to see how the product will fly in the retail arena. This process allows us to balance an outside perspective and additional ideas from both of these audiences before making a final decision on the concept. It also helps to drive timelines, because the team is working toward consumer research dates or major retail deadlines on the calendar.

With the product concept now well understood, we become a little more methodical in our approach to ensure we hit our quality, time, and margin targets. Line trials are done to make sure we can manufacture efficiently, and press checks are performed to be certain our creative vision comes to life. Zookeepers (project managers) direct the process by making sure the right conversations are happening, the tough questions are being asked, and people are being held to task. Weekly Product Council meetings involving every operational and product development function kick in, giving us more cross-functional perspective and allowing us to address any issues that emerge that jeopardize our timing.

Insourced brains, outsourced machines. A key element of this process is an integrated team, in-house, that includes representatives from each of the major product-development and operational functions. By vertically orienting the intellectual property in-house, we build a tight and cohesive team. Keeping those people working together for a number of years only enhances the quality of the product experiences we can deliver. Walking around our office, you will find teams of experts in fragrance, formulation, engineering, and industrial and graphic design, just to name a few. Through our people, we uphold the belief that by seeking out and assembling the greatest craftspeople in each field and setting them up to do what they do best, we're able to make great product experiences consistently. This is essential, because execution is where products often go from good to great. Or more commonly, compromises occur that turn them into dogs. Having a close-knit group of experts who work on a product from conception to execution means we can take advantage of late learning to improve a product in the final steps and overcome unexpected hurdles that could otherwise compromise it.

Above all else, throughout the entire production process we try to keep one question at the forefront of our minds: Is this a product we would want to use ourselves? This helps us lead the consumer, spark innovation, and avoid the me-too trap. At the end of the day, we create products that every one of our team members is passionate about. All the strategy and consumer research in the world can't make up for passion when it comes to delivering great experiences.

ERROR AUTOPSY: BURSTING THE BUBBLE MYTH AND TRYING TO WIN IN DISH

Not a lot of people walk around wishing they could find a better dish soap. And yet, winning in dish has been a personal obsession since our second year in business. This product plays to the strengths of our experience pillars: It sits out on countertops where design is a factor, fragrance is a huge part of the experience, and nontoxicity is especially important in a product you submerge your hands in. But it is an incredibly hard category to disrupt. Two brands have dominated this category for decades and with razor thin margins and low prices, there is not much opportunity to elevate the opportunity.

Our first dish soap, packaged in a container designed by Karim Rashid in 2002, helped put us on the map, but failed to deliver the experience we had hoped. Beautiful, iconic, and functional, it created a better experience by dispensing from the bottom, eliminating the need to flip the bottle over every time you squirted. But it was an innovation in the formula that flew in the face of one of the unbreakable rules of dish soap: More bubbles equals more effective.

Observing consumers in their homes washing a dish once and rinsing it again and again, we came to the belief that the biggest problem with doing dishes was the time it takes to rinse the bubbles off. Formulas were designed to be so foamy that they made the entire process of doing dishes longer and also wasted a lot of water. Knowing that bubbles have nothing to do with cleaning power (we know you don't believe it, but it's true), we decided to add an ingredient that would make the formula fast-rinsing. You'd get the bubbles you wanted, but when you started rinsing, they'd quickly disperse to leave you with just a sparkling clean dish. Well, consumers hated it. They equated bubbles with clean, and even though we had made their lives easier and their dishes just as clean, the process of rinsing and rinsing again was what told them the formula was powerful. It didn't matter that the bubbles were purely cosmetic, they wanted them. Our goal of delivering a great experience fell flat. We eventually reformulated, and even today, our dish soap is sudsier than it really needs to be. Maybe some-

pin •————→ butler •————→ leaf •————→ pump

▲ **DISRUPTING DISH.** Reinventing a very basic product has been an ongoing battle. We think we finally got it right but let us know.

day we will start a campaign to educate the world on how unhelpful those little bubbles really are. Just another potential battle in the fight against dirty.

MUSE: RICHARD BRANSON, VIRGIN

Stepping onto a Virgin America flight is like stepping into an iPod. From the minute you check in and receive the passport-size boarding pass (why didn't someone think of this sooner?) to the time you place your order through the food-on-demand system, you know that Virgin America has truly improved the flying experience. One of Branson's many customer service successes, Virgin America proves that little things can add up to big things—from lavender ambient lighting (easy on your eyes) to self-serve water at the back of the plane (convenient and there when you want it). Personally, we think one of the best touches is the Method soap in the bathroom—now anyone can enjoy a mile-high Method hand wash!

To hear Richard Branson talk about all of this, it seems so simple. "We are bringing back a little glamour to flying," he says. And why not? In an era when every other carrier is focused on cutting services and charging more fees, even a little glamour goes a long way. And it's yet another reason we've been students

▲ **WE ARE ALL IN THIS TOGETHER.** Teaming up with the people's champion of delivering better product experiences.

of Branson's ever since Eric sent the Virgin Group an unsolicited pitch letter to launch Virgin water. We're still waiting for a reply. But we digress . . .

Perhaps above all else, we stole courage from Virgin—the courage to take on a Goliath in a tired category and offer an alternative rooted in a better experience. We did it just once; Virgin's done it dozens, if not hundreds of times. We're inspired by that sense of adventure, cheekiness, fun, and irreverence. Richard Branson reminds you that the hardest part of taking any entrepreneurial challenge is just having the courage to be different and stand up for what you believe.

obsession

7

DESIGN
DRIVEN

build design leadership
into your dna

We don't have a good language to talk about this kind of thing. In most people's vocabularies, design means veneer. . . . But to me, nothing could be further from the meaning of design. Design is the fundamental soul of a man-made creation.

—Steve Jobs, CEO of Apple

FROM THE FIRST HUMAN TOOLS AND THE EARLI-est cave paintings to the construction of the Egyptian pyramids and the rise of Greek architecture, people have always been able to recognize iconic design when they see it. Not surprisingly, the design IQ of the average person has never been higher than it is today. From the enduring columns of the Parthenon to the prescient sketches of Leonardo da Vinci to the minimalist utility of the iPhone, the role of design in the life of the average individual has only grown broader and deeper with each new generation.

If our grandparents competed in the age of mass production and our parents competed in the age of information, today's entrepreneurs compete in the age of aesthetics. Want a pair of custom Vans kicks? Design them yourself online—they'll be at your door in less than three weeks! Personalized M&Ms, printed with your own custom messages? Simply log on to mymms.com, pick your favorite color, and fill in the blanks. Thanks to designer collaborations at discount retailers, we can now expect high-end and customized design at all price points—from Vera Wang mattresses at Target to IKEA's praised minimalist Scandinavian designs at cut-rate prices. Even current media trends reflect a broad interest in better design: Flip on the tube and you're as likely to catch an episode of *Extreme Home Makeover, Martha Stewart Living,* or *Project Runway* as you are a sitcom or major-league game. Never before has design been more mainstream—or more mystifying.

It's not that we misunderstand design; it's that so many of us now have our own unique understanding of what design means. Few words in the English language are as confusing as *design*. Look it up in *Webster's* or the *Oxford English Dictionary* and you'll find dozens of definitions. Google it and you'll get close to 2 billion page results. Even Wikipedia, the crowd-sourced online encyclopedia that seems to have an answer for everything, fails to reach a consensus on the meaning of the word, stating, "No generally-accepted definition of 'design' exists."

This is particularly true throughout the various disciplines of the business world. Inventory management, sustainability, research and development—even within the same company the word *design* will have many different meanings. To the marketing team, it may refer to the graphic layout of a new magazine ad or billboard. To the guys in IT, design has to do with software engineering and Web analytics. Ask the head of HR about design, and you'll likely hear about human capital development, labor mobility, and concurrent occupational structures. Confused yet? From person to person and industry to industry, design is in the eye of the beholder.

Inevitably, misconceptions about design abound. Design has become associated with the supermodel, the creative genius, and the expensive. Design is New York, but not New Jersey. Design is "iconic," that is, symbolic and not real. Design is mysterious and elite, not something any average person can enjoy. But when used intelligently, design has the power to heal our world and change our lives. We just have to understand it first.

OUR VIEW OF DESIGN

When we talk about design, we're not just talking about aesthetics design—the style and ergonomics of a given product (though we'll get to that). We're also talking about system design—the underlying, often unspoken intentions that dictate how a business forms and achieves its goals and creates a positive impact in the world.

Take Toyota's *kaizen* philosophy. Japanese for "continuous improvement," *kaizen* is a system that empowers everyone in the company to contribute innovative ideas by inviting feedback from blue-collar workers on the production line, sales reps in the field, accountants in the offices, and anyone else in the company. In contrast, back in the United States, the Big Three American car companies' allegiance to the status quo caused them to lose touch with their founding intentions—guiding principles like innovation, efficiency, and value.

We're sons of automotive entrepreneurs, so Detroit's decline was a daily concern at our families' dinner tables. Stagnating under layers of "safe" business strategy, Detroit suffocated the dynamic design thinking that had made it successful in the first place. The grand era of automotive design that had given rise to triumphs like curvaceous Corvette fenders and Cadillac's iconic fins—a time when all of popular culture looked to Detroit for innovative technical and aesthetic cues—had faded into the past. Decades of compromises, from cost-cutting measures to risk-averse leadership, had resulted in a collection of largely uninspiring look-alike brands and me-too models.

In retrospect, the reason for Detroit's resistance to innovation is obvious: The American automotive industry was no longer designed for "continuous improvement." Quite the opposite, in fact. After nearly a century of global dominance, American carmakers had grown risk-averse and complacent. Underestimating the threat from their Asian competitors, they were inclined to inertia and recalcitrance instead of innovation and resourcefulness. Change was considered a liability. Throughout the industry, the mantra was the same: "If it ain't broke, don't fix it" (local mechanics excepted, of course).

The status quo strategy made sense at the time because the popular business thinking called for focusing on the here and now, analyzing the most recent benchmarks, and minimizing risk in the short term. And yet as the challenges mounted in the 1970s and '80s, it became clear that Detroit didn't simply have a fuel-efficiency problem or a reliability problem. Rising fuel costs and viable foreign competitors were only symptoms. Detroit had a design problem.

When we launched our own company two decades later, the fall of Detroit was still fresh in our minds. We resolved not to make the same mistake and recognized that the democratization of design in its many forms was a cultural shift that could give us a major competitive advantage. We were intent on designing not just our products, but our *company*—to create innovation predictably and consistently, again and again, and to continually improve it with every decision we made so that those innovations could not only create a competitive advantage, but also a positive impact on our world.

As Tom Peters often preaches, design is why you most frequently love or hate something. We love TiVo because it is well designed. We hate Comcast's DVR because it is so poorly designed. Sooner or later, every touch point of a brand—from products to customer service to marketing—has to be designed. So why do so few companies make design a priority? We've been asking ourselves that for years. As our seventh and last obsession, we have devoted ourselves to being design driven from the very beginning.

PUTTING IT ALL ON THE LINE FOR DESIGN

When we started Method, we each funded it with $45,000 of our own money, allowing us just $90,000 to take an idea from a sheet of paper to a product on store shelves. Wrestling with that challenge, we spent almost half our seed capital just figuring out our packaging design! Crazy? Maybe. Obsessed? Absolutely. It's a fine line sometimes.

Of course, there was method to our madness. When we looked at brands that cut through the clutter, we noticed a common theme: The best of them used a unique packaging format and created a new product archetype. Altoids had the tin box, Absolut had the minimalist bottle, and Red Bull had the slim can. The design solution was clear: Our spray cleaner needed an iconic shape of its own. Unsatisfied with all of the available prefabricated bottles, we designed one ourselves, based on a camping fuel bottle we found in Norway, and hired San Francisco–based graphic designer Michael Rutchik to create the labels. The original images featured Eric's girlfriend alongside Adam and props from Home Depot—a sink, kitchen counter, and window frame (we kept the receipt and returned it all immediately after the photo shoot). Using the last pennies of our meager life savings, we toiled over design from the get-go. With the bottle ready and the last of our money invested in formulation, we knew our packaging would have to do our marketing for us. As history has shown, it did.

That's one of the things we love about design—it's one of the few business tools that is both immediate and impactful. Design has the power to instantly change perceptions by engaging our emotions and seducing our senses. Method wasn't the first to realize this, of course. Our culture is full of clichés that demonstrate the power of appealing design—"love at first sight," "seeing is believing," "a picture is worth a thousand words." When harnessed the right way, design has the power to transform a commodity into a special, memorable

▲ **CLUTTER CUTTER.** As the world gets more complex, simple design gets rewarded.

product experience. People in business so easily forget that we are all humans selling to other humans, who are by nature tactile, visual, and emotional creatures. We are motivated by brands and products that give us sensory pleasure, and we respond strongly to our surroundings through unique experiences. At Method, part of our strategy is to deliver great experiences by designing for the senses, which make our products a heightened experiential part of everyday life. Our ultimate goal is to elevate everyday soap into an object of desire.

This was our thinking when we hired Karim Rashid, hailed by *Time* magazine as "the poet of plastic." We designed our first dish soap during year one at Method, and we needed to make a statement—declaring to the press, investors, and retailers where we were taking the home-care category. In a lot of ways, it was similar to how an automotive or apparel brand launches a concept car or halo product—one lasting impression creates room for countless others.

So why Karim? Eric created a list of the most famous industrial designers in

▲ **KARIM RASHID, THE POET OF PLASTIC.** When launching a new company or brand, search for a design collaborator.

the world (remember, "Always knock on the big door"), and we planned to work our way through each name until someone said yes. Karim was first on the list because we knew he was committed to democratizing design by creating for the majority, not the minority, and we wanted to dispel the myth that good design is too expensive for the average person. So we shot him an e-mail titled "Are you our design genius?" in which we pitched the idea of reinventing the banal world of dish soap with a revolutionary design. Shocking us both, he e-mailed us back within twenty minutes, and we struck a deal to pay him with a combination of cash and company stock.

With Karim we made a deep commitment to industrial design, to create not just unique packaging but unique products—and that tradition continues. For a small brand, this is a major investment that eats up capital, but it's one we feel necessary to ward off fast followers and threats from private labels. Leveraging industrial design places us in a unique position. The capital expenditure involved in custom designs makes it harder for copycats or private-label brands to imitate us, while the speed with which we create products makes it difficult for competitors who operate on enormous scale to follow quickly.

Ten years later, our obsession with design hasn't wavered (though we have a little more cash to work with now). In fact, it's only gotten stronger. After working with Karim for many years, we've since brought design in-house, cultivating a design-centric company, and putting design work side by side with the rest of our business. Every employee can see exactly how our designers function and understand the role design plays in the overall vision we have for the company. To us, design is a way of thinking—a way of imagining and creating the future that every Method employee participates in. At Method, everyone is asked to think like a designer, whether concocting a formulation or solving an accounting issue. In making design a core focus of our company, we've come up with certain steps to make sure that—no matter your industry—you can build a culture focused on design.

LEVERAGE DESIGN PLUS BUSINESS THINKING

Entire books could be dedicated to the art of creating healthy tension between the creative and the business mind, and over the past few years, we've certainly experienced a lot of drama in the pursuit. Building a utopia where brilliant business managers and creative geniuses work side by side in complete harmony is as likely as opening a unicorn ranch in the clouds. Trust us, we've tried (the former, that is). Despite our best efforts, we've never found this magical place—though we have learned some of the secrets to creating an environment where both managers and creatives thrive.

Most companies treat design as something to be handled by a small group of people—generally toward the bottom of the organization's hierarchy. This mystifies us. We challenge you to find a company that leverages design as a core competitive advantage without creative leadership at the highest ranks of the company.

Method is no exception. Internally, we preach the need to integrate design and business thinking. In essence, business thinking is about being skilled at decision making—working from a set of existing options to create predictable and reproducible systems that are, ideally, bulletproof. In other words, good business thinkers are great at making decisions based on *existing* knowledge— things that have worked in the past. And in business, once something is working, it seems prudent to copy it. The result: systems that are reliable, but not always original. This is business as algorithm—quantifiable, measurable, and provable.

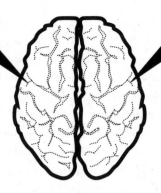

BUSINESS THINKING	DESIGN THINKING
decision making from a set of existing alternatives	*creating new choices, drive differentiation*

▲ **BLURRING THE LINES BETWEEN STRATEGY AND CREATIVITY.**
Design thinking is about creating new choices that drive differentiation.

It's a philosophy that speaks to the management belief "What gets measured gets done."

Design thinking, however, is just the opposite—it's about creating new choices, options that didn't exist before. The goal of design is to create something new, better, or different.

There's a reason that design thinking is so different from more traditional ways of thinking. Most people use inductive reasoning (drawing general conclusions based on many observed particulars) and deductive reasoning (drawing particular conclusions based on accepted generalizations) to consider a problem or come up with an idea. But designers also rely on a third type: abductive reasoning—the logic of what might be. This is the art of creating something that's never been imagined before. The vocabulary isn't important, but the underlying concept is: Designers don't copy, they create. While an engineer may study problems and devise solutions from a known set of tools, designers must imagine solutions that don't come from a preexisting set of techniques—forcing themselves to create wholly original and unpredictable solutions to problems. You see where this leads, right? It leads to solutions that are novel and unique, which, if harnessed appropriately, are powerful tools in business, sustainability, and culture.

The fact that business and design require different ways of working is why most creative and design resources live in outsourced design firms and advertising agencies. If you're managing a reliable and predictable process, you will tend to attract folks who are skilled at creating a predictable result time and again. Just imagine the power of harnessing these two different approaches into one fluid team—one that simultaneously and artfully balances rigor and discipline with disruption and innovation. This has been our goal since the beginning.

And from the beginning, we've worked together as cofounders to bring these two approaches together. We aren't the first to try this; companies that blur the lines between design and business thinking very often put an artist at or near the top with the operators. Consider the heyday of Motor City. When U.S. automakers were at the vanguard of the industry, they had artists in leadership positions. At GM, the visionary Harley J. Earl's GM Tech Center, designed by Eero Saarinen, was the world's most modern and complete industrial design center when it opened in 1955, and it influenced some of the world's most notable car designs. Over at Ford, while Henry was the visionary founder, and his grandson Henry II rebuilt the brand into a powerful industrial force following World War II, the most creative of the family was the founder's son Edsel—a design genius who was responsible for the Lincoln Continental and other unique Ford styles during the Art Deco period of the 1930s.

Today we live in a burgeoning age of corporate design heroes who understand design's value. VPs of design and chief design officers are becoming more

▲ **DON'T OUTSOURCE YOUR SOUL.** At Method, design not only is insourced, but also has a seat at the leadership table with people like Josh Handy, our Disruptor, aka head of innovation. (Doesn't he look like Moby?)

prominent and more powerful players within the executive suite, and design itself is taking on as important a role as marketing and executive leadership. Design will always be subjective—it can't be managed by committee—so companies need a cultural leader at the top who gives the company an aesthetic point of view and ensures that the organization stays on track. Ultimately, while you need to weave design and business thinking through the entire organization, one person needs to be responsible for championing, curating, and editing the brand's visual point of view.

To achieve this balance throughout Method, we have reinforced our leadership team with two VPs who have design backgrounds—our VP of product design and our VP of brand experience—who work hand in hand on a daily basis with our CFO and VP of operations. Method would not have lasted this long if it had operated inefficiently, and while not celebrated as often, those who work in the more traditional roles in operations and finance form the backbone from which the consumer experience grows. So while part of Method runs the way you would expect a consumer-products company to run, with strong operating rigor (mixing soaps, manufacturing pumps, filling orders, etc.), the part that defines the experience for the consumer and creates every touch point of the brand feels more like a design firm than a manufacturer.

Managing the juxtaposition of creative innovation and operational predictability is a constant challenge for us and our entire leadership team. It means balancing discipline and disruption, left brain and right brain, in productive, not destructive, ways. We need to give people the freedom to follow their gut, but we also need to hold them accountable for their performance. So we set a high bar, recognizing that occasional failure is an unavoidable side effect of pushing into uncharted waters. While we have to do everything possible to wow our advocates, we know we also need to eliminate unnecessary costs and inefficiencies. Which is to say, we need to be equally skilled at quantifying the now and intuiting what's next. Of course, how many companies are truly good at that?

One important benefit of bringing design in-house is that it allows you to move faster. By not having to deal with outsiders, you can skip the process of bringing your partners up to speed or explaining a concept. Production challenges can be dealt with swiftly. An in-house team lowers creative and design cost, whereas paying an agency's project fees or retainers can be exorbitantly expensive. Designers help you envision what can be, and the tools of prototyping allow you to share your vision with others. In-house design allows you to more efficiently exploit every touch point to maximize marketing effectiveness. More-

▲ **WE LIVE THROUGH DESIGN.** At Method every floor is the design floor. Design is not a function. It's what we do.

over, designers and creatives tend to be eclectic and passionate, bringing positive influences to the culture. Below are more ways to make design a focus of your company.

BUILD A DESIGN COMPANY, NOT A DESIGN DEPARTMENT At Method, design is a philosophy, an attitude. You will never hear us say the words *design department,* because as in the case of our obsession to be a green giant, we expect everyone to think like a designer to influence every molecule of our business. Take our first laundry presentation in the United Kingdom by our head of sales. Faced with his first big sales call on a yet-to-exist account in a hypercompetitive market, he needed a way to bring creativity to what, for the buyers he was meeting, was just another laundry presentation. So instead of a PowerPoint deck, he set up a clothesline in the buyer's office, writing out the important content of his pitch on pieces of laundry. Businesses today have to not only outthink the competition, but also outimagine them, which means thinking more like designers. And what happened in that laundry sales presentation? Yup, we got the green light!

Design at Method is naturally a creative process, but that isn't to say design is limited to strictly "creative" disciplines. Take technology—even minute changes to the hardware and software we use to operate our distribution net-

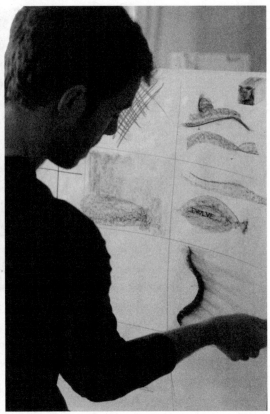

▲ **METHOD ART SCHOOL.** A designer is anyone who makes something better so we encourage everyone to think like a designer.

work are best made with an eye toward creative solutions. And for all the creativity that goes into fragrance design, at least as much creative energy goes into determining the most efficient way to get that particular fragrance from the other side of the world into each of the rapidly moving bottles on our automated production line. Because such problems permeate our business, we make sure that everyone at Method is a designer.

Operating under this broader definition of design, we challenge our team members to exemplify the designer's mind-set in all of their work—be it identifying innovative improvements in their own specialty (like a procurement manager uncovering an elegant cost-saving means of sourcing new materials) or even spotting a solution outside their field (as when a team member in sales discovers how to stack and ship our products in a more sustainable manner). As you might expect, divas and dilettantes don't last long in the face of so much creative cross-pollination, no matter how talented they are. But in a corporate world that's in love with e-mail memos and PowerPoint slides, a design-centered outlook helps keep everyone fresh and focused on the power of the original idea. Creativity comes in all forms, in many types of people, in many lines of work and ways of life. The key is to harness, cultivate, and enhance this natural creativity in every discipline. Once you can do that, you're designing.

One tool for helping everyone think like a designer is an office space that encourages this type of thinking, literally building collaborative behaviors into the culture. While in advertising, Eric saw firsthand the influence and connection between office-space design and the work that was created within it. While working at Fallon McElligott in Minneapolis, Eric noticed that the company went to great lengths to design an amazing space that inspired creativity and made collaboration flow like water. Years later, while he was working at Hal Riney in San Francisco, the company moved its offices to a new custom-built space whose designers had lacked an understanding of how office design connects to creativity. The office felt more like a glorified accounting firm, and it sucked much of the energy and creativity out of the company. This contributed to the demise of a once great agency.

From our earliest days working out of Adam's car, we believed our office design would have a profound effect on the quality of the work. There is a fine interplay between architecture and humanity, and stepping into our lobby, you immediately understand that design is a priority for us. The modern furniture and exposed brick walls are more evocative of a boutique hotel than the offices of a soap company. More important, all the materials are recycled or reused and LEED (Leadership in Energy and Environmental Design) certified. Unlike companies that put creative effort only into the design floor or department, our entire company feels like the design floor, including our satellite offices. The offices are designed to raise the bar on the quality of work and subconsciously remind everyone of the importance of design. They are yet another physical realization of our philosophy of style with substance. In essence, the Method office space, by having a great design, demands great work.

Besides inspiring us, well-designed offices also encourage brainstorming. We don't believe that scheduled, structured brainstorming sessions yield the best ideas, and with the pace of work today, finding time to brainstorm becomes more and more difficult. In its place, we prefer a company in which brainstorming is a natural part of the entire day and where ideas are continually being shared, vetted, and built upon in short ideation loops. Essentially, work should feel like one giant brainstorm.

We view design as extroverted experimentation—from our boundless whiteboard surfaces throughout the office (wiki walls) to the open floor plan that keeps everyone's work in plain sight. Features like these create the vibe of an open lab, where ideas are free to be shared, debated, and improved. Our designers (and that includes the formulators) post their work on the walls so everyone who passes by can be influenced by it and can help build upon it. We put up whiteboards not just in the conference rooms, but also in the hallways and around workspaces. This process encourages our employees to build upon, not merely critique, other people's work. The work that is shared is unfinished, but just sharing it creates a place where we receive constructive input from everyone, not just a few people.

The challenge with this way of working is that designers are uneasy about placing new, fragile ideas into the harsh sunlight for all to see. Doing so requires trust—trust that the organization will help the ideas become bigger and better rather than focus on flaws: "Yes, it's a good idea, and here is how to make it better" instead of "Yes, it's a good idea, but here's the problem." This requires constant practice, reinforcing behaviors that we believe define effective collaboration:

▲ **OUR WIKI WALLS.** Make design the first step, not the last step.

- Assume goodwill. If you start from a common goal, you'll build first and critique later.
- Ask questions. The fastest way to kill collaboration is to try to answer questions. We force ourselves to ask them instead.
- Demonstrate understanding. Help people align their interests so they'll use two minds, not just one, to create something new.
- Communicate directly. Trust us, you can't do anything new via e-mail.
- Be supportive. "Yes, and," not "Yes, but."

Another way we help everyone think like a designer is by distributing our design guidelines (which internally we refer to as brand behaviors) to the entire company. By educating everyone on our approach to design, we ensure that everyone understands the importance of design as an asset and of maintaining a unified design vision. Once, a buyer at a major grocery chain gave a sales director a hard time about the lack of benefits listed on the front of our daily shower cleaner. Because our sales director was educated on Method's design philosophy, he could help the buyer understand that the lack of visual clutter actually helped it stand out on shelf and made our advocates more likely to leave it in the shower, making the product more convenient to use. Ultimately, the whole company has to buy into design for it to be successful.

Good design is good business.

—**Thomas Watson, former president and chairman of IBM**

INVEST MORE IN DESIGN AND LESS IN STRATEGY In our MBA-saturated culture, strategy-based thinking tends to overshadow design- and idea-based thinking. Wary of the big idea, investors would rather bet on the big strategy, no matter how unoriginal it is. We've seen companies spend hundreds of thousands of dollars on strategic reports from big consultancies like Bain or McKinsey, only to balk when the same experts advise investing fifty grand on new product outside their comfort zone. But a poor strategy well executed is always better than a great strategy poorly executed. After all, consumers don't see the strategy; they see the execution.

What consumers see, feel, taste, and experience is what they remember. And this is the result of what we do, what we execute, not the strategy behind it. For example, Virgin America's strategy is probably no different from that of

Alaska Airlines; the difference is the creative execution of the brand and in-flight experience—and what a huge difference. After all, consumers don't buy Power-Point documents. They buy the product, the result of all the design decisions that have gone into it. Imagine a wife yelling to her husband during the commercials, "Honey, quick, get in here! There's a great strategy on TV!" Don't get us wrong, we're definitely guilty of occasionally dropping a simple thought into the middle of a triangle on a PowerPoint slide and calling it "strategic thinking," but there's a limit.

The good news is that we live in the design age. But we also live in the age of accountability. Today, no business decision gets made without in-depth analytical data and clear proof points about its impact on the bottom line. The new corporate mantra is "If you can't measure it, you can't manage it." It's hard to assess the emotional impact of design on the success of a business, but we believe design drives return on investment, making it one of the few tools that create a tangible statement for your brand or business with every dollar you spend. A common thread in any company that successfully uses design as a competitive advantage is the unwavering belief that good design makes good business.

Over the years, there has been some compelling data that we may be guilty of overusing to our board to justify design expenditures. The London School of Economics found that on average, every $1 spent on design yielded a $3 ROI, and packaging design guru Rob Wallace has preached that on average, every dollar invested in package design generates over $400 of incremental profit within CPG companies. Whichever number you believe, our proof is empirical; we've vaulted to leadership status in one of the biggest industries on the planet by investing in design—and we've done it profitably.

Understanding ROI from design is challenging because great design has an emotional impact on consumers that is inherently hard to measure. Great design is also about great consumer experiences through every touch point, so pulling apart different aspects of a design for testing is inherently flawed. For years we would debate the role of design, and often some among us would argue that design is not needed everywhere. For example, team members understood the value of design on a hand wash that assumes a decorative role on the sink but less so its value on a toilet-bowl cleaner, which will probably get shoved in a cabinet no matter how beautiful the bottle. Our argument is that if we are going to be design driven, we need to take every opportunity to elevate design for a higher experience for the consumer. If you break that promise in any one spot,

▲ **THE DESIGN BECOMES THE ADVERTISING.** Great design creates great advertising and social media engagement.

the entire design experience of your brand falls apart. Great design is in the details.

MAKE DESIGN AN ITERATIVE PROCESS Design is an iterative process— one in which you move quickly from observation to idea to execution to learning, repeating the process in quick loops until the concept becomes highly evolved and refined. At Method we brief, design, prototype, and repeat quickly, as many times as it takes to land on the right solution. Sometimes we get it right on the first try, and other times it can take twenty tries. Traditional companies follow a longer, linear process. Our system allows collective thinking to occur in a fast and furious way to overcome problems and barriers that block innovation.

Designing iteratively requires making design the first step, not the last. We expect creatives to bring business thinking to the table, and we expect our talented business people to participate in creative thinking at the very beginning. A linear, business opportunity–led approach limits the ability of ideas to build upon one other in iteration cycles. Most companies take a waterfall approach where you move development between stages, and the designers enter late in the process. Our creative process not only can begin before a brief is written, but we encourage it to. Our goal is to bring all that problem-solving design goodness to the front end. Frequently the creative inspires the strategy, not the other way around. Having a culture in which everyone is trained to think like a designer enables this asynchronous but highly productive methodology, because each person knows the brand inside out and is in tune with the business direction and the audience it serves. The goal is to close the gap between strategy and execution so that we can drive a vision, go fast, and surprise consumers.

An example of this creative method is our collaboration with Disney. When Disney approached us, instead of first engaging in a long process of business and legal due diligence to decide whether or not to proceed, we made the design the first step. The strategy was simple: Find a design solution for a kids'

▲ **INNOVATION IS CREATIVITY APPLIED TO BUSINESS.** Design helps us envision the future and can change our perceptions of what's possible.

line of products that played to both kids' and adults' sensibilities. The kids' market has always been very challenging because there is a small window before the primary purchase decision transfers from the adult to the child, and finding a product that can transcend this transfer is elusive. This is why character licensing dominates this aisle. While characters may delight a child, they leave many parents less than thrilled about having gaudy SpongeBob on their kitchen counter or the questionable ingredients a product may contain.

Creating a kids' line with strong sensibilities that would satisfy the desires of both a child and an adult was no easy task. But when our designers and Disney's design studio crafted the first concepts on how Method and Mickey could come together, we began to understand the vision. Our studio created a prototype from their original ideas, and within weeks, after several loops of observation, prototype, learning, and reapplication, we landed on a design that achieved our goal. Only at this point did we begin proving the business case, which moved quickly because we had a tangible idea and vision in hand that everyone could see, touch, and understand. The result was a design that evoked the iconic

▲ **THIS IS NO MICKEY MOUSE HAND WASH.** Equally loved by kids and adults.

Mickey silhouette that kids love, but with a minimalist graphic treatment that adults would equally love in their homes.

FOCUS DESIGN ON SOLVING CONSUMER-CENTRIC PROB-LEMS Great design begins with asking yourself, "What problem am I trying to solve?" We frequently use People Against Dirty as our opening brief for a specific design challenge. When we set out to disrupt laundry for the second time, we started by asking what type of "dirty" we should rid from the world of laundry? Luckily for us, there were many monsters that needed slaying in this category. In this case, we set out to rid the world of the ubiquitous and obnoxious laundry jug. The laundry jug is the SUV of the consumer products industry. It's heavy, it's messy, and it's wasteful in terms of the resources it uses, but it's supremely profitable for its makers. Framing the problem correctly led us to think differently about laundry detergent and ask the question, "How can we eliminate the mess for consumers while fundamentally changing the relationship between laundry detergent and the environment?" This led us to a hunch: What if we created a single-load laundry pill that could easily be popped into your machine with no waste or excess packaging? Genius, right? Well, sort of. After a year of prototyping, we were getting really close but couldn't quite get the price

▲ **FAILURE OFTEN OPENS A NEW DOOR FOR SUCCESS.** By failing to create a laundry pill we found a way to reinvent the ubiquitous laundry jug. But eventually our green chefs will crack this too.

and cold-water solubility to a place where we were 100 percent comfortable with the product's experience and economics.

After yet another round of trying to create our magic pill, we finally declared the project a big fat failure. But by going down this unique path, our green-chef team had created a formula that was amazingly concentrated (because it had to fit in that pill), so we started asking ourselves what else we could do with this formula. Could we put it in a pump? The team quickly put our miracle formula in a cosmetic pump that is usually used for baby-diaper creams and antiaging serums—not ideal, but it gave us a sense of the experience. Now we were onto something. We tried it at home, we gave it to friends and neighbors, and we asked, "Would this change how you do laundry?" Within a couple of weeks, we had created several more rounds of prototypes and sent them to a small group of consumers. We invited them to share their experiences, and the feedback was consistent. Everyone was skeptical when they received it in the mail (how can this little pump ever work?), but after they tried it, they did not want to give it back. Within a couple of weeks, we had gone from idea to consumer auditions, and we quickly aligned as a team to go for it. The idea for the design of the bottle came fast because we already understood the benefits the product should communicate to consumers. There was no testing of different shapes and no lengthy and

▲ **PEOPLE PARTICIPATE IN PACKAGES.** Great design invites engagement.

expensive design process. The shape shattered the traditional archetype for a laundry detergent, and the design gave us a means to challenge the category. Bye-bye, jug. Hello, Method laundry.

All told, the pump and formula stability took a circuitous two-year path to market, but the big idea hatched in an instant. In 2010 our laundry pump won the Industrial Design Society of America's Best in Show IDEA (Industrial Design Excellence Award), an honor normally reserved for "sexier" products like iPods

---

MASH IT UP—GREAT DESIGN HAS TENSION

While great design requires a single goal or vision, truly great design often unites many opposing design tensions. This underlying tension is what gives great design uniqueness, energy, and excitement. Look no further than mash-ups, which have become commonplace in fashion and music. High-end designers like John Varvatos partner with Converse, and musical artists like Jay-Z and Eminem often collaborate on other pop stars' work even if their style is completely different. The more unexpected the mash-up, the more exciting it is.

Cirque du Soleil is a great example of using a mash-up to reinvent the circus. Producers bring together world-class performing art and knee-slapping street entertainment. The result is a show that you love and respect—a combination that we would argue is the essence of any great brand. Our original mash-up—style and substance—created a new archetype and experience for cleaning products. Advocates love the fact that our designs are beautiful and fun, and they respect us for our commitment to sustainability and human health. Even our original pitch to Target—"designer commodities"—was a mash-up of two opposing ideas from opposite ends of the consumer spectrum.

The challenge of mashing up two opposing ideas is that the hybrid is often hard to successfully shepherd through the maze of consumer focus groups and executive committees. We combined a personal-care-style pump dispenser with laundry detergent or hand soap, then mashed up that mash-up with sea-mineral fragrance from the world of cosmetics. Fortunately, if you mash up two things that already work together, you can use each as a proof point to convince others why the new mash-up might succeed.

---

and motorcycles. It also grabbed a 2011 Good Housekeeping VIP (Very Innovative Products) award, but most important, it changed an industry and drastically improved the environmental footprint of laundry detergent. Seriously, if you decide you want to try one of our products after reading this book, try our laundry detergent. It's the best product we've ever made.

ERROR AUTOPSY: BLOQ, OUR EDSEL

Years ago, when we tried to launch into the personal-care category, we were faced with a major design challenge. How do we break in? How do you disrupt a space where almost every imaginable bottle shape, color, and ingredient has been created? You can't out-Dove Dove or out-Olay Olay.

We knew we had to do something truly unique, and our home-care designs weren't going to cut it. The result was Bloq, an übernatural personal-care line of products that was packaged in an iconic square shape. Bloq brought a lot of innovation to the market, with high-quality natural formulations and interesting, unexpected fragrances never before seen at mass market—not to mention unique features, bar-soap-like texture, and packaging that not only stood out on the shelf but fit neatly together with other products like part of a Lego set in your shower and bathroom. Stepping back, we believed Bloq really brought something different to the category. We were right—just not in the way we'd hoped.

Despite our innovations, Bloq bombed. Big time. While the bottle was beautifully designed, the underlying business design of the product was rushed and somewhat happenstance. It blew a hole in our 2008 financial plan; the cost of marking down the product to clear it out of the marketplace sank our P&L that year. It was the first time we learned that killing a new product could be much more expensive than launching one. Worse, Bloq crippled our ability to spend just as the recession picked up steam and direct competition took dead aim at the green category. The timing could not have been worse.

Fortunately, we learned more from the Bloq failure than we would have learned from two years in business school. (Unfortunately, it was a lot more expensive than B-school tuition.) Nevertheless, the failure of Bloq taught us once and for all that design is about much more than aesthetics alone.

Mistake #1: Letting the business drive the brand instead of the brand drive the business. We got into the body-care business for business reasons only: The category was big, operationally synergistic with our cur-

▲ **BE A REBEL WITH A CAUSE.** The best work
always dances on the edge of embracing us, which
was the case with our bloq personal-care line.

rent model, and it had attractive margins. Plus, the success of our hand
wash meant that retailers were pressuring us to expand our body-care
line. The thing is, our brand was structured to disrupt home care with a
personal-care approach ("Aveda for the home"). Taking it into body care
lacked a big idea to disrupt—one of the keys to all of our best successes.
Hand soap was successful because we linked it to consumers' relationships with their homes (decor), not just their feelings for skin care. Bottom
line, the Method brand belonged in the home.

Mistake #2: Lack of alignment. To find a big idea for the category, we
had to push design hard. The idea was to appropriate the trend of "object
design" from the world of fine fragrance and bring it to body care. Initially, we wanted to create a bottle that, like a smooth river stone, would
not stand up but would sit in your shower or bath. We also wanted it to
be merchandised in bins rather than on the shelf. As we went to cut steel,
our team couldn't get aligned around the idea of merchandising in bins.
So we changed course at the last minute to a block shape that (we thought
at the time) disrupted the curvy world of body wash. It behaved like an

iconic object but could still sit on shelves. This was not a good kick-ass-at-fast moment. The totally square shape was hard to mold, so, under the pressure to meet our launch dates, we ended up working with the only blow molder in the world that would attempt it. As a result, the production line ran slow—and it was located in a plant far from our filler. Compounding problems of slow production and long supply lines, we decided to do each bottle in a different color and silk-screen pattern. Instead of working from common platforms, each Bloq SKU was its own unique noninterchangable item, making logistics with shippers, stockers, and shoppers a headache.

Mistake #3: Launching a big new product on a large scale without beta testing it first. The combination of a less-than-strategic supply chain and a big forecast led to huge inventory levels. So when Bloq launched and didn't sell well, we were sitting on too much inventory to make quick improvements and correct our mistakes. Soon enough, retailers started to discontinue it, marking down the price and hitting us with huge financial liabilities.

In the end, we had to give away the finished-goods inventory and recycle thousands of expensive, perfectly decorated bottles that had never been filled. It forced us to lay off employees, and it wiped out our marketing budget for the year. Although we learned some valid lessons from Bloq, we remain steadfast in our commitment to taking big risks—but from now on, we'll do so with our design principles at the top of our minds.

MUSE: ANDY SPADE, COFOUNDER OF KATE SPADE

Andy Spade—cofounder of Kate Spade with his wife and business partner, Kate—is one of our personal masters of design and a major muse. Andy started his career in advertising before taking the leap into launching his own. (Andy also happens to be the brother of comedian David Spade, a fact that should give you a sense of his personality; picture someone with the design sensibilities of Calvin Klein and then add a high dose of comedy.) Probably the closest comparison to Andy is the movie director Wes Anderson, who combines great style with a quirky personality. We were very fortunate to have Andy and Kate as early investors, and they have served as an ongoing source of inspiration ever since.

It's no secret that Eric has a bit of a man crush on Andy, and as Eric's wife

▲ **ANDY'S ADVICE** . . . the bigger you get, the smaller you need to act.

likes to say, Andy is the only person other than Eric who shows up at social occasions with a PowerPoint deck of new ideas. We also share a passion for Napa and a fine red wine. Andy is a constant creator of new ideas and loves casually brainstorming the way other people love eating. His energy and optimism are highly contagious, and those are two things that entrepreneurs like us need a steady diet of when trying to go up the mountain.

Our take on appropriation was inspired by Andy, who shared with us something he learned from his advertising friend Rich Silverstein: "Everyone borrows from the past. Just don't steal from other competitors. Find inspirations from the world of art, architecture, or other distant worlds and put them together in a new way."

The most important thing we've learned from Andy is how to manage the aesthetics of a master brand that spans multiple categories. A brand like Method can be a design challenge, as it covers distinct categories with unique functions and consumer motivations. Andy told us to be sure everything always feels the same but never looks the same. In other words, manage for coherence, not consistency.

We have always been awed by Andy's ability to humanize a brand and bring to it a personality that connects with people on an emotional and spiritual level. So we hired him and Kate to collaborate with us on our first laundry line, with the goal of bringing fashion sensibilities to the drab world of laundry.

Andy has taught us the power of brands that show humility and don't try to be all things to all people. He also showed us that brands whose developers have soul and follow their own intuition actually get better as they grow bigger, rather than becoming watered-down versions of themselves. In essence, the larger you grow, the smaller you must act. How are we doing, Andy?

CONCLUSION

SAYING GOOD-BYE

go forth with purpose—a really great ending full of awesomeness that we hope inspires you

SITTING DOWN TO WRITE THIS CONCLUSION, WE couldn't help but think, *Shouldn't you be drawing your own conclusions from the book?* We've spent over two hundred pages giving you all of the wit and wisdom we have to offer, and you want *more*? Sure, we could synthesize all of our genius ideas and inspiring stories into nice little bullet points for you, but you've already read them. Why not make better use of this space?

But our editor wanted us to give you a proper send-off rather than just forcing you to let yourself out, so we decided some sort of closing would be in order. Really, if there is one thing we want you to you take away from this book it's . . . buy our soap. Lots of it! Make your friends buy it too. Put it in strangers' carts at the grocery store. Come on, we need your help!

OK, if there are *two* things you take away from this book, here's the second: Find your own obsessions. Discover what drives you. Bring a higher purpose to your career and your life. Over the past ten years, we have learned that the joy and rewards of building a business are magnified a thousand times when they're tied to a higher purpose or social cause. Gordon Gekko may have been right when it comes to the selfish rewards of greed, but he got it wrong when it comes to building a fulfilling career. It's human nature to want to be a part of something bigger than ourselves. It makes us happier. If you aren't inspired by a bigger purpose in life, you will eventually burn out and fall short of your potential. We've seen it in our employees—who will generally go somewhere else if they don't love what they're doing—and we've felt it ourselves.

Having a mission drives people, and it drives culture. Working for the common good helps everyone put ego aside and work collaboratively as a team. That said, building a shared vision around a mission takes a different leadership style. It's about spiritual management instead of micromanagement. Today's entrepreneurs and cultural leaders motivate with purpose, asking, "Why are we here?" They help others see the bigger picture. At a recent offsite, we asked all present to talk about what motivated them. While money was important, it was not the chief motivator. (After all, if money was our core focus we would be trading stocks, not selling soap.) Instead, we talked about pursuing a purpose greater than profits—the big picture. Each of us came to Method to make the world a cleaner place. It may sound soft, but this passion is a competitive advantage because it draws the kind of talent that big, soulless corporations can't attract. And by helping people see the bigger picture, we bring out the best in our employees. Here's what we are most proud of: starting a business with a social mission to do good in the world. Creating a mission-driven company is the right thing for society and the planet, and it is becoming the best thing to do for the bottom line. Some of the trends we discussed in this book—such as operating in an era of media transparency and making green selfish—will only continue to give mission-driven companies a competitive advantage over their larger, old-style competitors. We challenge you to find your own social mission, and we recommend harnessing social media to help the process along. If you haven't discovered it already, finding your social mission will transform your business into an agent of change.

We also challenge you to let go of strategy now and then. Strategy alone is not enough to succeed. Look deeper. Find your own obsessions. Obsess over the fun stuff, like culture. We think you'll find it more inspiring (as will your employees). Obsess over the tough stuff, like your competitive advantages. We think such obsessions will help you really understand what distinguishes you from everyone else. And once you've started obsessing, let us know! Send us your ideas and obsessions anytime at eric@methodhome.com and adam@method home.com and feel free to include pictures or jokes. After all, we've told you everything we know, and we could use some new material for the next book.

—Eric and Adam

THANK YOU!

To anyone who has become a **Person Against Dirty** and brought one of our products into their homes. You have spread our mission and built our business, and we promise to never let you down.

To all the people who have worked at **Method** over the past ten years. You are the business and our inspiration.

To all of our **investors**, including Steve Simon, Herb Simon, Tim Koogle, Scott Potter, Robbie Rayne, and Bob Boughner, who all put their money where their mouths were and funded this revolution. We salute you!

To our **manufacturing partners**, who help make Method every day. We appreciate your taking the leap and going the extra mile.

To our **parents, wives, family, and friends,** who did everything they could to support us on this fantastic journey. You are the foundation of our lives and our success.

To **Michael, Craig, David, Jim, Steve, and all of our early vendor partners,** who were generous with their skills without the promise of payment. Thank you for helping making Method possible.

To **Lucas,** our writing partner, who helped a couple of writing rookies create a book that we could truly be proud of. We look forward to doing it again.

To our **rock star designers Deena and Stephanie, and Daniel at Portfolio,** thank you for lending us your talents and time to create this beautiful book.

To our **editor, Brooke,** who championed our writing and was ever so patient with our missed deadlines while we were busy making soap.

To **Mel,** our agent, for being a Person Against Dirty and making us feel cool when we say, "Talk to my agent." We hope we made you proud in the end.

We could not have done it without any of you! Thank you!

INDEX

fabric softeners, 86

Facebook, 65, 67, 79, 85, 144, 154, 189

failures: creating success through, 148; design and, 218, 228–30; laundry pill as, 228–30; personalizing sustainability to inspire change and, 104; small and cheap, 146–48; transparency about, 104. *See also* error autopsy; mistakes

Fallon McElligott, 221

fast. *See* "kick ass at fast"/speed

feedback: culture and, 41; inspiring advocates for your social mission and, 81; "kick ass at fast" and, 146; about laundry pill, 229; living in state of make and, 146; organization/structure at Method and, 81; product experiences and, 202; retail relationships and, 174; shift from paid to earned media and, 69

field trips, 108–9, 171

fieldwork, 110

firing/laying off employees, 24–25, 153, 233

Fishburne, Tom, 134

Fisher, Don, 5

Fiske, Neil, 166

flat is fast, 151–52

flatpaks, 123–24

"follow the hour hand," 155

Ford Corporation, 217

Ford, Edsel, 217

Ford, Henry II, 217

Forrester Research, 194

fragrance/smell: Adam and Eric's discussions about starting a business and, 6; appropriation of, 199; cultural shifts and, 8; culture and, 43; design and, 220, 230, 231, 232; Humanifesto and, 73; inspiring advocates and, 85; kick ass at fast and, 147, 148; leaky bottle problem and, 21; personalizing sustainability and, 105, 106; product experiences and, 184, 191, 192, 195, 196, 197, 199, 200, 202, 203; retail relationships and, 171, 172, 177

Franken, Al, 89

Franklin, Aretha, 138

Fraser, Drew, 50

Freedman, Andrea, 40

Frey, Don, 51

fun: in cleaning, 7, 75–77; culture and, 36, 37, 43–44, 53, 56, 60, 240; design and, 230; finding obsessions and, 240; and Hirshberg/Stonyfield Farm as model, 125; Humanifesto and, 73; inspiring advocates and, 66; personalizing sustainability and, 100; product experiences and, 187–88, 205; retail relationships and, 167, 176

Gandhi, Mahatma, 117

Gap, The, 5

Gates, Bill, 5

Gen Y, 72

General Motors (GM), 200–201, 217

Germain, Dan, 91

Gilliam, Terry, 40

Go Naked, 177

golden ylang-ylang rule, 73

Good Housekeeping VIP award, 231

goodwill, 46

Google, 33, 41, 154

"graduation strategy," 175

Graham, Nicholas, 75

Graves, Michael, 15, 177

greed, 99–101, 239

green/green movement: and competitors launching of green products, 23; consumer apathy as threat to, 96; decision to focus on cleaning products for Method and, 4–6; first product failure at Method and, 23; Humanifesto and, 73; as irrelevant, 95–96; and making green selfish, 100–101; mission-driven companies and, 240; mission of, 101; pitching Method products and, 9; as revolution, 95–96

greenskeeping, 106–11

greenwashing, 95–97

Gretzky, Wayne, 143

grocery stores: product experiences and, 183

growth: as addictive, 135; collaboration and, 46–47; culture and, 34, 35–36, 39,

PORTFOLIO
/ PENGUIN
Published by the Penguin Group
Penguin Group
(USA) Inc.,
375 Hudson
Street, New York,
New York 10014,
U.S.A. • Penguin
Group (Canada),
90 Eglinton
Avenue East, Suite 700,
Toronto, Ontario, Canada M4P
2Y3 (a division of Pearson Penguin
Canada Inc.) • Penguin Books Ltd,
80 Strand, London WC2R 0RL,
England • Penguin Ireland, 25 St.
Stephen's Green, Dublin 2, Ireland
(a division of Penguin Books
Ltd) • Penguin Books
Australia Ltd, 250 Camberwell
Road, Camberwell, Victoria 3124,
Australia (a division of Pearson
Australia Group Pty Ltd) • Penguin
Books India Pvt Ltd, 11 Community
Centre, Panchsheel Park, New Delhi—
110 017, India • Penguin Group (NZ), 67 Apollo
Drive, Rosedale, Auckland 0632, New Zealand
(a division of Pearson New Zealand Ltd) • Penguin
Books (South Africa) (Pty) Ltd, 24 Sturdee Avenue,
Rosebank, Johannesburg 2196, South Africa

Penguin Books Ltd, Registered Offices: 80 Strand,
London WC2R 0RL, England

First published in 2011 by Portfolio / Penguin, a member of
Penguin Group (USA) Inc.

10 9 8 7 6 5 4 3 2 1

Copyright © Eric Ryan and Adam Lowry, 2011
All rights reserved

Photograph and drawing credits
Pages 19, 103, 187: © Stan Musilek • 24, 53, 56, 60, 91, 111, 120, 140, 145, 167,
199, 204, 217, 220, 222, 226, 228: Photographs by Stephanie Lachowicz Art •
59: © 2011 Zappos.com, Inc. or its affiliates • 68: James Wojcik • 70: Nathan Aaron,
methodlust.com • 86: Photograph by Martin Wonnacott, represented by Cake
Factory • 107, 122, 147, 191, 198, 213, 225, 227: Photographs by Steve Epstein Art
• 126: Stonyfield Farm • 134: Illustration by Tom Fishburne, marketoonist.com •
152: © 2011 www.nickonken.com • 155: Stefanie Keenan • 205: Droga5 • 214: Karim
Rashid, Inc. • 229: Photograph by Jay Ganaden • 234: Anna Thiessen

LIBRARY OF CONGRESS CATALOGING IN PUBLICATION DATA
Ryan, Eric.
The Method method : seven obsessions that helped our scrappy start-up turn an industry
upside down / Eric Ryan and Adam Lowry ; with Lucas Conley.
p.   cm.
Includes index.
ISBN 978-1-59184-399-3 (hardback)
1. Business planning. 2. Strategic planning. 3. Method (Firm) I. Lowry, Adam. II. Conley,
Lucas. III. Title.
HD30.28.R927 2011
658.4'012—dc22   2011015069

Printed in the United States of America   Designed by Daniel Lagin with Deena Moore

method

hand wash

sweet water

12 FL OZ (354mL)